CONFESSIONS OF A
RECRUITING DIRECTOR

CONFESSIONS

of a
Recruiting Director

The Insider's Guide
to Landing Your First Job

BRAD KARSH

To Kelly

PRENTICE HALL PRESS

THE BERKLEY PUBLISHING GROUP
Published by the Penguin Group
Penguin Group (USA) Inc.
375 Hudson Street, New York, New York 10014, USA
Penguin Group (Canada), 90 Eglinton Avenue East, Suite 700, Toronto, Ontario M4P 2Y3, Canada (a division of Pearson Penguin Canada Inc.)
Penguin Books Ltd., 80 Strand, London WC2R 0RL, England
Penguin Group Ireland, 25 St. Stephen's Green, Dublin 2, Ireland (a division of Penguin Books Ltd.)
Penguin Group (Australia), 250 Camberwell Road, Camberwell, Victoria 3124, Australia (a division of Pearson Australia Group Pty. Ltd.)
Penguin Books India Pvt. Ltd., 11 Community Centre, Panchsheel Park, New Delhi—110 017, India
Penguin Group (NZ), cnr. Airborne and Rosedale Roads, Albany, Auckland 1310, New Zealand (a division of Pearson New Zealand Ltd.)
Penguin Books (South Africa) (Pty.) Ltd., 24 Sturdee Avenue, Rosebank, Johannesburg 2196, South Africa

Penguin Books Ltd., Registered Offices: 80 Strand, London WC2R 0RL, England

Copyright © 2006 by Brad Karsh
Text design by Kristin del Rosario
Cover design and art by Jill Boltin

PRINTING HISTORY
Prentice Hall Press trade paperback edition / April 2006

Prentice Hall Press is a registered trademark of Penguin Group (USA) Inc.

Library of Congress Cataloging-in-Publication Data

Karsh, Brad.
    Confessions of a recruiting director: the insider's guide to landing your first job / by Brad Karsh.
        p. cm.
    ISBN 0–7352–0404–7
 1. Job hunting. I. Title.
    HF5382.7.K38 2006
    650.14—dc22

                                                                2005058694

PRINTED IN THE UNITED STATES OF AMERICA

10 9 8 7 6 5 4 3 2

To my wife, Lisa,
the love of my life

ACKNOWLEDGMENTS

Most authors acknowledge all the people who helped them write the manuscript and ultimately publish the book. In this case, though, I really did most of the work, so I'm not sure anyone should be acknowledged. Okay, just kidding! As a chronic procrastinator with moderate writing skills, I find it a miracle this book ever was written. The following people played a huge role. I would like to thank . . .

Julia Moskin and Darren Kapelus for giving me the idea and the support to even consider writing a book.

Matthew Carnicelli, an agent extraordinaire, who taught me how to write a proposal, and then managed to get it accepted.

Christel Winkler and the staff at Prentice Hall Press who did everything and more to make the book a reality.

Josh Bellin for serving as my own personal (unpaid) editor for more than twenty years. From proofreading stories of genetically engineered mutants taking over the world to fixing my tendency toward the prolix, he's corrected it all.

Willie Wilkov for always giving it to me straight—even when the truth hurts.

Courtney Pike for organizing, editing, cutting and pasting, and being my new grad sounding board.

Brad Zibung for the PR base that helped make the book even possible in the first place.

My father, Paul, who truly made me believe that I could do anything in the world.

My mother, Letty, who always pushed (in a loving way) me to go for it. I'd still be playing cards on the family room floor if it weren't for her.

My brother, Murrel, for being my supporter and entrepreneurial role model.

And most importantly my wife, Lisa, who inspires, supports, and cares for me, and is the inspiration for all of my happiness.

CONTENTS

Behind Closed Doors in the Recruiting Department

Let's be honest. Nobody really likes looking for a job. In fact, it probably will rank up there as one of the most painful experiences of your life. I'm guessing you don't come back from class on Friday and say to your roommate, "I'm so psyched! I'm going to spend all weekend job searching. I just can't wait!"

But the fact of the matter is you have to get out there and start looking, unless you happen to win the lottery, or you want to spend the next few years sleeping on your parents' couch.

It's perfectly understandable that job seeking isn't on the top of the fun-stuff list. Indeed, if you're like most students, you probably are doing everything in your power to avoid it. But here's the good part. There are companies out there that are going to pay you tens of thousands of dollars just to have you work for them. Crazy but true! It's actually a pretty good deal.

That's the purpose of this book: to help you make the transition from college student to working professional, and to find that dream job that will make you happy, motivated, and fulfilled, and, by the way, also pay you tens of thousands of dollars!

There's no "magic formula" or quick fix. It takes hard work and perseverance and even a bit of luck to land a job. But knowing how the game is played and knowing how to win the game makes the process easier, quicker, and definitely more successful.

Confessions of a Recruiting Director will unveil the inside story of how to land your first job. You won't believe what you learn about how candidates are selected and how companies make the decision to hire college students. You'll hear firsthand how recruiting directors look at candidates just like you and determine if you get the job or if you get the rejection letter.

From the moment you click "send" on your computer or mail off the resume, what happens? This book will reveal the entire hiring process from the inside, so you know exactly how to land the job of your dreams. You'll finally get the inside scoop on:

- What recruiting directors are looking for in their fifteen-second resume scan
- Why you should spend sixteen hours networking for every hour you spend job searching on the Internet
- The tricks of the trade to write a cover letter that actually gets read
- What's going on in the mind of an interviewer
- Why a thank-you note could end up determining if you get a job or not
- How and when to follow up on a job without coming off like a stalker

If you're like most students, you've received job-search advice from all sorts of people: your parents, your friends, probably even your dentist's cousin's golf partner. But chances are you've NEVER received advice from a recruiting director—literally the person who ultimately decides if a candidate gets the job or not.

As you well know, getting that first job out of college is no easy task. And since you've never had a full-time job before, you certainly don't know how to get your first one! While your friends and parents may be well intended, they simply don't have the expertise and perspective on what it takes to get that first job. Just because they have a job doesn't mean they know how recruiting directors make the hiring decision. That's like saying just because you've ridden a horse, you can win the Kentucky Derby.

This book will give you the first-time-ever perspective of a former recruiting director. You'll learn the inside story, you'll discover what goes on inside the walls of a recruiting department, and you'll get the absolute latest on trends and changes in the industry. In short, you'll now know what corporate recruiting directors know.

Recruiting directors and recruiting departments can take many shapes and sizes. At some companies that hire hundreds of college students annually, the recruiting departments typically employ dozens of recruiters, hiring managers, and human resources professionals—all dedicated to finding great college students. At smaller companies there may be just a few folks working in recruiting and maybe none dedicated specifically to college students. And finally, some organizations have no recruiting department at all, but rather bosses are simply responsible for finding their own employees.

No matter what size, shape, or name a recruiting director (or hiring manager or HR professional or boss) takes, each one shares this in common: all are sifting through scores of resumes and cover letters, interviewing dozens of candidates, and trying to find the perfect match for the company. They are all looking at resumes like yours, interviewing candidates like you, and determining who will get the dream job and who will get yet another glorious rejection letter.

That's what makes this book special. You'll finally get the straight deal—right from a former recruiting director—on what will get you hired. You will be amazed at the advice in this book. *Confessions of a Recruiting Director* is very different from what you've heard in the past. But unlike everything else you've been told, this comes directly from the source. It's like a backstage pass to the entire recruiting process (but without the delightful food spread).

The book is divided into six sections that outline the basic components of any job search: resumes, networking, interviewing, cover letters, thank-you notes, and sealing the deal. Not only will you learn what to do and why to do it, but you'll also learn what NOT to do. We'll show you before AND after resumes and cover letters, we'll talk about the right AND wrong things to say in an interview, and we'll talk about the correct AND incorrect ways to handle your job search.

In each section you'll read "Shocking Confessions" about how recruiting directors practice their craft and how they decide who gets the job and who doesn't. No doubt this will be new information to you that will help you with the job search. Also critical is how to take those

"Shocking Confessions" and apply them to help you get a job. Again, that's the intent of *Confessions of a Recruiting Director*—to tell you the inside story and then give you the advice on how to "beat the system."

Everything in this book is real, tangible, and applicable, right from the recruiting director's perspective. Upon finishing this book, you'll have a very specific plan to land the job of your dreams.

Good luck and happy reading!

Resumes
Your Life in Fifteen Seconds

Fourteen Shocking Resume Confessions
from the Recruiting Department—
and the Ten Mistakes That Drive It Crazy

Help Wanted: Financial Analyst, The Goldman Sachs Group, Inc.:

As a recent college graduate, you may be considered for an analyst position at Goldman Sachs. Analysts learn a great deal about our businesses, develop important relationships, and build the skills necessary to carry them through to the next level of their careers. Most analysts enter a division at the firm through our two-year analyst program. At the completion of the two-year programs, some analysts remain with the firm while some choose to pursue other opportunities, such as business school.

At Goldman Sachs we rely on everyone to add to our success. Early in your career, you will be working directly with senior client executives and side by side with some of the finest, most respected experts in our firm.

Required skills:
  College degree
  Strong quantitative skills
  Economics/Finance background
  GPA of 3.5 or above
  College leadership position

Please submit your resume to jobs@goldman.com.

Click.

You did it. You just sent off your resume for the job of your dreams. No doubt Goldman Sachs has been anxiously awaiting your resume and can breathe a heavy sigh of relief. You can probably hear the celebration in the boardroom: "Guess what? Josh Bellin has finally applied to be a financial analyst at Goldman Sachs!! At last, he's ours!"

Can you sense the sarcasm in that last statement?

Shocking Resume Confession #1
Fifty percent of resumes submitted for jobs are never read. By anyone. Ever.

You're probably thinking, "But that's not fair! I'd be a great financial analyst at Goldman Sachs!"

You might be. But it doesn't matter. That's simply not the way the game is played.

Part of the reason that's so disconcerting is that it's pretty much the opposite of your last big application process: getting into college.

When you apply to college, most admissions departments consider every applicant individually. At some schools, they spend hour upon hour on your file and then debate your credentials in sessions with a staff of ten admissions counselors.

In the real world your resume is probably sitting in some big stack on somebody's desk, or in some computer database, unread.

The reason isn't that employers are trying to be devious or malicious. It's simply a function of time and money (isn't everything these days?).

There are always way more qualified candidates than there are entry-level jobs. When the economy isn't humming along, the situation is even worse.

Take Microsoft for example. They receive upwards of 20,000 unsolicited resumes a month, not to mention how many they get when they actually post a job opening. That's not uncommon at other big, popular companies. Even at smaller companies, a help-wanted ad can generate 1,000 resumes or more. Now think about the math: If Microsoft spent even five minutes looking at each and every resume and cover letter, that would mean 100,000 minutes a month doing nothing but looking at unsolicited resumes. That's 1,666 hours, or ten people working full-time at forty hours per week for the entire month. It's simply not going to happen.

And again, even 1000 resumes, at five minutes per, is eighty-three hours of review time. The economics of today's business world do not support a recruiter doing nothing but reading resumes for two solid weeks for every job opening.

You may be thinking, "But isn't that the job of a recruiter—to read resumes?" Yes, it is, but it's only a fraction of what they do. In fact, recruiters typically spend less than 10 percent of their time reading resumes.

Alas, there's no way to know which companies do read all their resumes and which ones don't. But know that either way, spending a huge amount of time reading resumes is not the top priority of any recruiting department.

Shocking Resume Confession #2
Even if someone does read your resume, he or she will likely spend about fifteen seconds looking at it.

Fifteen seconds. It's scary. Your entire life merits just fifteen seconds of someone's time.

This mercilessly brief review time is based on two factors: the limited amount of time a recruiter has to look at resumes and the reviewing adeptness one gets from reading so many.

Nevertheless, it's a frightening proposition. Four years of college, all of your internships, jobs, extracurricular activities, leadership, and more, and someone sizes you up in fifteen seconds!

So what are recruiting directors doing in their mysterious fifteen-second scan? Let's clear up the mystery. They are looking for someone who:

- Goes to a good school
- Has excellent grades
- Is involved in a variety of activities
- Has shown commitment and leadership in those activities
- Has relevant internships or jobs

These points aren't in any particular order because every recruiter will look at these experiences differently. But rest assured these are the types of attributes that virtually any company is looking for in a new employee.

However, don't freak out if you don't have a 4.0 from Harvard, weren't captain of the basketball team, and don't have a White House internship on your resume. And similarly, don't think that just because you were president of your class, you'll get a job anywhere you please.

Shocking Resume Confession #3
There is usually not a single entry on your resume that will either guarantee you a job or prevent you from getting a job.

Recruiters are looking for "the package" but recognize that there is no such thing as a perfect candidate. They take a holistic view of your resume to make sure to capture the essence of who you are (in fifteen seconds!).

For instance, just because you had a great internship does not mean you will necessarily get an interview. The competition is fierce and the positions are few. Similarly, just because you didn't have a great internship doesn't mean you won't get an interview.

Think about it this way. Darren and Julia are two candidates for a full-time job in the account management department of advertising agency Young & Rubicam.

Darren had a great summer internship at Ogilvy and Mather advertising in New York before his senior year. But Darren didn't go to a particularly good school, he has a low GPA, he wasn't involved in any campus activities, and he has no leadership skills or experiences.

Along comes Julia. She has no internships. In fact, she's only worked as a waitress the past three summers. But she went to an excellent school, has a wonderful GPA, was president of her school's American Advertising Federation chapter, and was a member of the track team.

Julia's much more likely to get the interview based on the way a recruiter reviews a resume, assuming she's done a good job at presenting herself.

Shocking Resume Confession #4
No matter how strong the candidate, poorly written resumes get tossed in the trash can.

Remember: you have fifteen seconds to impress the recruiter who reviews your resume. You better make your resume shine. Sadly, in most instances, that's not the case for college students.

So what goes into a resume that shines? There are four main sections on every student resume:

- Personal information
- Education
- Experience
- Activities/Interests

PERSONAL INFORMATION

This is pretty straightforward. The personal information goes at the top of the page, not the bottom or on the side or in pretty little circles around the page. It includes your name, your address, your e-mail, and your phone number.

If you live on campus, you can include both your home address and your campus address. If you have different phone numbers for home and campus, leave each. Although if you have a cell phone, and that's the best way to reach you, just include that number on your resume. Here are a couple of examples:

One Address

Steve Hall
80 King's Way #11 • Paducah, KY 33117
612.895.8761 • stevehall@hotmail.com

Two address

Jeffrey Frishman
jfrishman@umr.edu

Campus Address
#1 Fraternity Drive
Rolla, MO 65402
612.798.3968

Permanent Address
138 Kilarny Drive
Greenview, IL 62246
618.690.4060

While this does seem pretty straightforward, students do manage to find a way to mess up this section when it comes to their e-mail addresses and phone messages.

Shocking Resume Confession #5
Companies do not want to hire studboy@yahoo.com or babe-a-liscious4@msn.com.

You wouldn't think that this would be a "Shocking Confession," but it continues to amaze me how often students use these e-mails on resumes and cover letters. Some recent classics that I have received include imsodamn-tired@gmail.com, thedirthead@yahoo.com, and spicychica2@msn.com (I guess spicychica and spicychica1 were already taken). Can you just imagine a recruiting director saying, "Hey, I really liked that guy Todd. Why don't you shoot him an e-mail at thedirthead@yahoo.com and have him come in for an interview. I love that name Dirt Head. I bet he's pretty nasty!"

Your e-mail address should simply be your first and last name, or first initial and last name, or even your first and last name with a number: paulfarmer21@hotmail.com. You get the picture.

Similarly, watch the answering message you leave on your phone. Somehow, "Yo dude, the Stanmeister, Chief, and Dougie Fresh are pounding some brewskies right now. Leave us a message and maybe we'll call you back when we're sober" doesn't seem like the best impression to leave. Again, I can't imagine the recruiter leaving a message like "Hello, Stanmeister, this is Brad Zibung from Smith Barney, and I would like to invite you to come to

New York for a full round of interviews—preferably when you're sober."

Your message should say, "Hello, this is Jeff Hiller. Thank you for calling but I'm not available right now. Please leave a message and I'll get back to you as soon as I can." Also, when you get a call, and you think it may be a recruiting director calling, answer by saying your name: "Hello, this is Jeff " or "Jeff Hiller."

As soon as you send out a resume and as soon as you begin the job search, you need to make sure you're acting like a professional and not a "wacky" college student. Certainly it's not as fun as the crazy messages and e-mails you used to be known by, but ultimately the goal is to get a job, and you need to show it.

After your personal information, you can skip the fluff.

Shocking Resume Confession #6
Summaries, profiles, and objectives are just wasted space.

Here's the deal. We talked about the fact that recruiting directors will likely spend a maximum of fifteen seconds looking at your resume. In that time they want to focus on what you've actually accomplished as opposed to reading why you think you're great. And, since you'll have a one-page resume, there really isn't all that much to summarize! Summaries and profiles are only options for people with at least five years of full-time work experience after college, and, even then, they are not a necessity. Summary/profile statements like "hard worker with ability to perform well on teams" or "two years internship experience at top engineering firms" are effectively worthless. First, anyone can write that they are a hard worker, and second, they can look down about four inches on your resume and see that you worked at a top engineering firm.

Similarly, objectives, especially when they talk about what YOU want from the job, are worthless. Do you think a company responds well to an objective statement like "looking to work for a dynamic company that will give me the opportunity to grow and to develop my skills"? First of all, who wouldn't want to work for a dynamic company with the chance to grow and learn? And secondly, do you think recruiting directors say, "Actually we are not a dynamic company, so maybe we should not hire Phil?

Or might they say, "Since Phil will be working for a bad boss, he won't have the chance to grow and develop his skills, so let's hire Amy. She doesn't want to grow or develop"? For even more on objectives and how to write a compelling objective when you do need one, check out page 35.

EDUCATION

So now that we've cleared up the mystery around profiles, summaries, and objectives, the first real section on your resume will be Education. As a student you always want to start with education. Even if you have great experience in the field you're entering, it's helpful to the readers to know that you're a student. Then they know when you're available to start working, even if you may still be in school and applying for an internship.

Here's what to include in the education section:

- School name and location
- Graduation month and year
- Degree
- Major/Minor/Concentration/Emphasis
- Dean's list/Academic honors, awards, or scholarships
- GPA
- Foreign study

Here's an example of a typical education entry:

Education

University of Central Michigan – Mt. Pleasant, MI, May 2006
- Bachelor of Arts in History, Journalism Minor
- Major GPA 3.8/4.0, Overall GPA 3.4/4.0
- Dean's List six of eight semesters
- College of Humanities Research Paper Honorable Mention Award, 2005

Wesleyan Program in Paris – Paris, France, Spring 2005
- Studied French history, architecture, and grammar in the native language

Notice the use of bullet points and bolding to make the section easy to read. Let's also talk about a few items listed here, as well as a few items that are NOT listed.

Other Schools

There's no need to list schools you may have transferred from, unless there's a significant accomplishment at one of those schools. All you need to do is list the school from which you've earned your degree. Also, if you're a senior, there's no need to list your high school (see page 36). Juniors, sophomores, and freshmen can list their high school but don't necessarily need to if they have other, more relevant items on the resume.

GPA

The general rule is to include your GPA if it's 3.2 or above, and don't include it if it's below. If your major GPA is higher, you can include it as well, but only if it's at least 0.3 points higher than your overall. There's no need to list "Major GPA 3.4, Overall GPA 3.3." If your major GPA is above a 3.2 and your overall isn't, then go ahead and just list your major GPA alone.

Finally, take advantage of a common mathematical phenomenon called rounding. I've received GPAs listed as 3.4823! Recruiting directors do not need your GPA carried out to the ten thousandth's percentile. You should round up, or down, according to the laws of mathematics. In other words, instead of 3.4823, simply list the GPA as 3.5.

The only exception is for those of you out there with a GPA at 3.95 or above, but not quite 4.0. In that case you don't want to round up to the proverbial perfection of a 4.0. You can simply put GPA 3.98.

Dean's List

If you're a frequent visitor to the dean's list, you can write it as we've shown in the example above. If you've only been on it once or just a couple of times, you can list it as

Dean's List Spring 2005, Spring 2006

Relevant Course Work

The question you need to ask yourself about relevant course work is "relevant to whom?"

Shocking Resume Confession #7
What you think is relevant and what a recruiting director thinks is relevant are two very different things.

Recruiting directors may care what your major is, and they may care what your minor is, but for the most part they care very little about what specific courses you took within your major. If you're a marketing major and applying for a job at a marketing company, a recruiting director is not going to say, "Well, Courtney took the Theory and Practice of Marketing, but not Advanced Marketing Principles, so we should reject her." Recruiting directors figure that you have a core competency and a strong knowledge within your major or minor. Now that doesn't mean you can go ahead and take a bunch of blow-off classes to breeze through your major. Oftentimes in an interview, you'll be asked questions about classes you took and what you learned.

The only time you want to list relevant course work is when your major does not match up to the field you want to pursue. For instance, if you are a history major and want to work in marketing, and you've taken a bunch of marketing courses, then you should list those classes to show the recruiting director that you have some experience and some aptitude in the field. In that case, simply list the marketing classes you've taken under the education heading.

EXPERIENCE

Quite simply, this is the most important part of your resume.

The experience section is largely where an employer determines if you have what it takes to succeed on the job. Yet many students sell themselves short in this section.

Shocking Resume Confession #8
Your experience section should include not only internships and work experience, but also prominent extracurricular and volunteer experience.

Most students think that if they didn't get paid to do something, it can't go in this section. That's a big mistake. Employers look at it totally differently. Their perspective is, if it was a meaningful experience that provided meaningful skills necessary for the job, then it's worth putting in the experience section, even if it was an extracurricular or volunteer position.

As a result, many student resumes will forgo great student club, fraternity/sorority, or even volunteer *experiences* outside the classroom at the expense of more mundane *jobs* like waiter, cashier, or babysitter. These resumes focus more lines, more attention, and better descriptions on jobs that quite frankly aren't nearly as important to the recruiting director.

Think about it this way. If you read a job description and you discover that the company is looking for leaders, and you happened to be president of the student government, don't you think that an employer would want to know that? The problem is, most students bury that experience under a separate section on their resume called "Other Experience" or "Extracurricular Experience."

Employers read a resume like you read an ad, top to bottom. As we've learned, they scan through resumes extremely quickly looking for candidates with relevant and compelling skills. If they don't find a match right away, they toss the resume. Thinking about it that way, you want to make sure you're listing your experiences from *most* to *least* important. Many times I received resumes that listed an experience section filled with jobs like sales associate, bartender, and library worker, and then *below that,* another section with a mention of a position like vice president of the senior class! Most recruiters won't even make it to the VP job before they throw away the resume.

Here's what you want to do. Look at all of your experiences including jobs, internships, extracurriculars, and volunteer work. Then look at the job description and match up what the company is looking for to what you've done. You want to list anywhere from four to six experiences in this section, in order of most important to least important for the job you're applying for. In some instances it may well be your internships that lead off this section, and in some instances it may be an extracurricular leadership position, but in almost all instances, the experience section will contain a combination of what you've done.

It's also important to list these experiences in order of most to least relevant to the recruiting director, regardless of chronology (see page 32). Again remember, with the limited time recruiters spend reading a resume, you always want to lead with the most important information.

When you list these experiences, make sure to include a few bullet points that describe your accomplishments in the position. Just ahead we'll look at an actual student resume and show you how to effectively write your bullet points, but here's how a typical experience section should look:

Experience

Promotions Director, WPGU 107.1FM, Champaign, IL, April 2005–April 2006
- Revamped remote broadcast process overhauling on-site logistics and improving client experience for up to 20 remotes per month
- Oversaw integrated promotional programs for clients including FedEx, Budweiser, and Hardee's
- Planned and executed "PGU Pre-game" tailgate party—station's largest event attended by more than 300 students and staffed by 75 station employees
- Launched department's internship program, enhancing training, evaluations, and work content for 20 interns
- Managed a staff of 20 for a 3,000-watt station covering 50 miles and targeting 70,000 18–34-year-olds
- Worked 35–40 hours/week while maintaining a full course load

President, Alpha Chi Omega Sorority, Spring 2005–Fall 2005
- Brought chapter finances from deficit to surplus by rewriting bylaws and overhauling financial operations
- Developed new house rules governing all activities for organization with 155 members and 55 live-ins
- Chapter selected as most improved out of 27 sororities on campus
- Won Andrea Levy Award given to one student out of 2,400 for outstanding service and commitment

Event Planner/Head Bartender, Cochrane On Daniel's, Champaign, IL, August 2004–May 2005
- Partnered with six social committee chairs to sell and plan several key bar events
- Oversaw a total staff of 50 student bartenders: 12–15/night
- Trained more than 50 new staff members, bartenders, and servers

Sales Associate, Adler Sporting Goods, Beachwood, OH, Summer 2005
- Won Employee of the Month for excellence in sales and service
- Ranked first out of five sales associates in summer sales
- Overhauled entire tennis department merchandising display, helping increase sales 7%

Notice the inclusion of the sorority leadership experience in this section, even though it's not considered a "job." Also notice that the entries are not necessarily listed chronologically, but rather from most to least important. I think you'd agree that this example does a great job in helping the recruiting director understand just how qualified this candidate is. You can also check out all the "after" resumes in the appendix for more great examples of how to format the experience section.

ACTIVITIES/INTERESTS

The final section on your resume should include a little bit about you to help round you out as a candidate. This section features a number of "one-liners" that cover clubs you've been involved in (where you didn't hold a leadership role), intramural sports, volunteer activities, language skills, and finally some of your interests. Here's how it should look:

Activities/Interests

- Public Relations Student Society of America member, 2005–Present
- American Cancer Society, Relay for Life participant, 2005–2006
- Leukemia Team in Training, Mayor's Midnight Sun Marathon Runner, Anchorage, AK 2005
- Intramural Softball, Volleyball, 2004–2006
- Interests include scuba diving, racquetball, travel, painting, and American history trivia

For the interest line, it's perfectly acceptable to list four or five of your actual interests, including one thing that might be considered a little "out there."

Shocking Resume Confession #9
A little personality on your
resume is a good thing.

Your activities and interests section can sometimes be a great conversation starter. I've seen entries like "*Cosby Show* reruns," "intensely spicy foods," and "James Bond fan" written in the interests section of a resume. In fact, I once interviewed a person who had listed "llama trainer" under this section! How can you interview someone with that on their resume and not ask them about llama training? It can make for a nice diversion.

Notice, though, that I said "a little" personality. Please don't go crazy, with interests like S & M, petty crimes, or foot fetishes, even if you do find them enjoyable! Remember, you are applying for a job; you're not filling out a profile for a dating service.

That wraps up the four main sections of any student resume. We've discussed what to put in the sections, what NOT to put in the sections, and the basics of ordering and format. We'll soon talk more specifically about the content of the main experience section.

When you ultimately put together your resume, it will take hours to make it just right. And as we discussed, a recruiting director is going to read the entire page in less than fifteen seconds. Now let's go behind the scenes to see what a recruiting director is looking for in an actual student resume during that infamous fifteen-second scan.

A REAL-LIFE EXAMPLE

Meet Lisa: Lisa Szabo is a senior at the University of Illinois. Like many, she was not too thrilled with the process of looking for a job. "I feel like I have done some decent things, but I'm not exactly sure how to say it," Lisa lamented. "It just seems unfair to have to cram my life onto a sheet of paper."

Let's take a look at Lisa's resume:

BEFORE

Lisa L. Szabo

LOCAL

123 East Main Street
Champaign, Illinois 61820-5666
(555) 123-4567 (Through May 2005)
lszabo@uiuc.edu

PERMANENT

123 Oxford Drive
Oak Park, Illinois 60477
(555) 987-4567 home
(708) 308-9715 mobile
lszabo@aol.com

EDUCATION

2001-present

University of Illinois Urbana-Champaign: May 2005
*Bachelor of Science degree in Speech Communications with a focus in Public Relations and Sports Management.

EXPERIENCE

June 2002- August 2002

Office Administrator, CivilTech Engineering: City of Chicago
*Responsible for all of the documents directed to Project Manager.
*Compiled, copied and distributed weekly progress reports for ongoing construction projects.
*Worked with Microsoft Works and Excel programs.
*Created progress spreadsheets.
*Facilitated communication between Project Manager, Assistant Managers, Engineers, and city of Chicago personnel.

April 2003-Dec.2003

Ticket Sales Representative/Promotional Activities Team Member, Chicago Bears Organization
*Generated ticket sales for the 2003 Bears season in Champaign, IL.
*Organizing and enacting promotional activities and marketing the Chicago Bears in Central Illinois.
*Assisted in the permanent seat license (PSL) campaign via fielding incoming phone calls, making outbound phone calls, and conducting customer service.
*Worked customer service booth on game-days to help field any
questions or concerns in regards to the Chicago Bears and ticket holders' experiences with the organization.

May 2004-August 2004

Public/Media Relations Intern, Joliet JackHammers Professional Baseball Team
*Assisted in the promotion of the team within the community and surrounding areas via team sponsored events, charitable events, festivals, school events, etc.
*Assisted in the preparation and coordination of pre-game and in between inning promotional activities, youth baseball camps, press conferences.
*Assisted in the creation, development, and coordination of community programs and school reading programs.
* Responsible for updating the team website to include current game and promotional give-away schedules. Also responsible for developing interactive features on JackHammers' website.
*Assisted in creation and development of press credentials and promotional flyers throughout season.
*Coordinated daily press box operation working with local, regional, & national media (ESPN); acted as a liaison for visiting and home team radio broadcasters.
*Gained experience in working with various other aspects of minor league baseball such as merchandising, ticket sales (corporate and regular season), and stadium operations.
*Worked with Microsoft Excel and Back Office (a website creation program)

continues on next page . . .

ACTIVITIES

August 2001-present   Member, Alpha Chi Omega Sorority

February 2004-present   Volunteer, Center For Women In Transition

References furnished upon request.

Lisa's applying for a job in sports management. She's a solid candidate, but this resume doesn't do a good job of highlighting her strengths. Here's my fifteen-second take on Lisa's resume:

1. **Lisa has some basic formatting problems.** This resume is more than one page and there's way too much white space on the left. Immediate red flag. Students *need* to have a one-page resume. There's not enough time to read more. In fact, some recruiters will actually throw away anything beyond one page. There's no need to list everything you've ever done, just what the recruiting director would find relevant.

2. **Lisa's education section looks like she has something to hide.** The University of Illinois is a good school and her major is relevant to the job, but there's no GPA. If there's no GPA, the reader assumes that's because it's not good.

3. **Lisa is not specific or explicit in describing her job experiences.** For first-time job hunters, this is the most important section of a resume. Recruiting directors will scan the headings to see what, if anything, is relevant, and then read the bullet points to find out what the student did.

   - Lisa's first job is not relevant to the job she's applying for. Even so, I quickly look to see what she did in case it's important or impressive. The first point says, *"Responsible for all of the documents directed to Project Manager."* Quite frankly, I have no idea what that means. For all I know, the documents were photocopies that she made, or perhaps she wrote hundred-page detailed reports for use with clients. It's so vague, and most recruiting directors get so many resumes, we just skip that point and move on. Incidentally, even though I wouldn't read them in my initial scan, the rest of the points on her resume are also so vague that they tell the reader nothing of interest. (Sorry, Lisa!)
   - The second job holds a bit more intrigue for me since it's in the sports field. But the way she writes about it is entirely generic. Her title is Ticket Sales Representative and her dates show she did the job in 2003. Her first point says, *"Generated ticket sales for the 2003 Bears season in Champaign, IL."*

     No duh! Generating ticket sales is what every ticket sales representative has ever done in the history of the profession!

If you read the rest of the points, they simply *describe* her job, as opposed to telling the reader what she actually *accomplished*. In fact, anyone who worked with her could write exactly the same thing on his or her resume.

- Her last job listed is, of course, the most important and the most recent, but for some reason she placed it third on her list. When I read this entry, it has more relevance to what Lisa wants to do, but it still can be dramatically improved.

   First of all, she starts four of the first five points with the word *assisted*. That's bad on two fronts. Obviously, you don't want to use the same word even twice as the lead bullet point word. Additionally, by saying "assisted," you downplay your role. In the "real world" very little work is done independently. Most projects are collaborative, but you don't need to write "assisted" or "helped" with everything you've done.

   Again, the first point sets the tone for the entry, and again it's very vague. She writes, *"Assisted in the promotion of the team within the community and surrounding areas via team-sponsored events, charitable events, festivals, school events, etc."*

   As the reader, I have several questions, How many events? What were your goals and what were your results? How many people attended? This entry simply does not give me enough information.

   For all I know, Lisa helped with two events attended by six people each, or she assisted with a gala 10,000-person event featuring the Queen of England! I just have no idea.

4. **The remaining points are structured similarly, with very little tangible detail.** There is an interesting reference to ESPN, but it's buried down in the sixth point, which I probably wouldn't read since it's so far down on the page.

The resume then ends with just two activities and, way at the bottom of the page, the ever-popular "References furnished upon request." Do you know anyone who has references that are NOT furnished upon request? Of course not. Everyone's references are available upon request.

There's no need to waste a line of your resume listing what is already obvious.

Based on the resume alone, it's highly doubtful that Lisa's resume would be selected for an interview out of a stack of hundreds of candidates.

Now, I certainly don't mean to be harsh or overly critical, but this is the way recruiting directors look at resumes. Most resumes are written this same way. And when you consider that recruiters typically review thousands of resumes a year, you can understand the approach.

From Lisa's perspective, she thought this was a pretty good resume. She knows what she did, so what's written on the resume makes sense to her. But to a recruiting director, it's remarkably vague. I really have no idea what she did to distinguish herself or to make a tangible difference in the jobs she held.

Here's the deal. With hundreds of resumes to choose from, a recruiting director is going to look for the "easiest" person to hire: someone who has proven abilities to do the job at hand and who has a track record of accomplishment. Recruiting company directors are searching out tangible, real-world skills that are transferable to their companies.

Sure, Lisa may have done some cool things on those jobs, but I don't have the time or patience to delve into it. I see what's listed on her resume and make my judgment in a few seconds. So when I read something like "Responsible for all of the documents directed to Project Manager," I simply assume that means nothing of relevance.

When looking at so many resumes, one tends to be cynical. If there's no GPA, then it must be bad. If she sold tickets, I'm assuming it's two tickets. If the point is vague, it must be worthless.

The good news for you is that most resumes are written the way Lisa wrote hers.

But there is hope. Now let's take a look at Lisa's revamped resume and you can decide for yourself if it looks any better. Same candidate, same experiences, just written entirely differently.

Lisa Szabo

lszabo@uiuc.edu

Campus
123 East Main Street
Champaign, IL 61844
217.123.4567

Permanent
31 Oxford Drive
Oak Park, IL 60477
312.945.3161

Education

University of Illinois–Urbana-Champaign: May 2005
Bachelor of Science in Speech Communication
Sports Management and Public Relations focus
Major GPA: 3.8/4.0, Overall GPA: 3.5/4.0
Dean's List: Summer '03–present

Experience

Joliet JackHammers Professional Baseball Team, Public Relations Intern, Joliet, IL, Summer 2004
- Managed all press credentials for two ESPN national news pieces as well as dozens of local media outlets
- Scheduled and coordinated more than 25 player and mascot appearances in the regional area
- Generated on-air mentions on WGN radio by initiating contact and securing relationship with station personality John Williams
- Executed tie-in promotion with Pepsi, selecting "Family of the Game" at all home contests
- Wrote four separate eight-page e-mail newsletters distributed to 2,000 season ticket holders, fans, and advertising partners
- Handled more than 200 charitable requests, determining and distributing team donations
- Organized and executed team's first-ever youth baseball camp with more than 40 participants
- Compiled and tracked all media mentions across print, broadcast, radio, and merchandise to help quantify stadium sponsorship
- Worked 70–80 hours/week to gain in-depth understanding of all team operations

Chicago Bears, Promotion Team Member/Ticket Sales Representative, Urbana, IL, 4/03–12/03
- Sold $60,000 worth of season tickets, mini packages, and group outings for Bear's 2003 season in Champaign
- Selected as one of eight interns from a pool of 300
- Fielded more than 1,000 calls on controversial Permanent Seat License (PSL) program for new Solider Field
- Manned customer service booth on game days, helping hundreds of ticket holders
- Worked 15 hours/week while maintaining full course load

City of Chicago–Civil Tech/Engineering, Office Administrator, Chicago, IL, Summer 2002
- Acted as key liaison to six engineer field managers overseeing weekly progress reports sent to head of Department of Transportation
- Scheduled more than 15 publicity appearances with Department of Transportation leaders and Aldermen for major publications like the *Chicago Tribune* and *Chicago Magazine*
- Uploaded, formatted, and organized digital picture archive for more than six ongoing city projects

Activities/Interests
- Speech Communications, Teaching Assistant, 2004–Present
- Women Against Domestic Violence, Volunteer, 2002–Present
- Alpha Chi Omega Social Sorority, Member, 2001–Present
- Center for Women in Transition, Volunteer, 2004–Present
- Interests include, sports, traveling, Roman history, and '80s rock

So, what do you think? Looks and sounds a bit better, doesn't it? Here's my take:

1. **The formatting has been vastly improved.** It's the first thing you notice. The resume just looks much nicer. It's easier to read, it's all on one page, and the white space is used more judiciously.

2. **The resume highlights her excellent academic record.** It turns out that Lisa has a wonderful GPA, and it's even stronger in her major. We obviously added it to the resume. She was also on the dean's list. Lisa just figured no one would care about her GPA. But the fact is, if it's not listed, the recruiter assumes it's pretty bad.

3. **Lisa's experience now appears impressive.** Of course we listed the JackHammers job first, but more important, look at how the entries all changed. Lisa got very specific about what she did, and she translated that into salient bullet points. We moved the ESPN bullet to the top, and we filled the rest of it with actual numbers and accomplishments:

   - 200 charitable requests
   - Tie-in with Pepsi
   - 25 player/mascot appearances

We even talked about how many hours she worked since it was so impressive. Employers are looking for students who have real-world skills and can hit the ground running. By mentioning ESPN, Pepsi, and even the sheer number of charitable requests, the resume paints the picture of a student who has been battle tested. For Lisa it was through an internship, but for many of you it could be through campus activities or volunteer experiences. Look at the company's job description and match the attributes they are looking for to the experiences you've had.

   - **The Chicago Bears job** now looks totally different. We talked about how much money in tickets she sold and even mentioned that it was a highly coveted job that only a few people got. These points send a signal to a recruiting director that this person is accomplished.

- For her job with the city, we made sure to mention that the publicity appearances she scheduled were for publications like the *Chicago Tribune* and not just the *Tinyville Monthly*.

4. Finally, the resume ends with some activities and interests that show she's a well-rounded individual.

I think we can all agree that the new resume is substantially better. However, the trick is not to merely copy what we've done for Lisa on your resume.

Shocking Resume Confession #10
Your resume needs to be different and distinct from everyone else's, based on your education, experiences, activities, and the specific job you are pursuing.

In addition to Lisa's resume, this book is filled with amazing resumes in the appendix. You'll quickly see that it's not going to work to simply copy these resumes for your own (sorry!). Like a fingerprint, every resume is going to be different based on what you've accomplished and what you want to do. For some students their education is stellar, and they'll want to highlight that. For others, maybe it's a slew of amazing internships or meaningful jobs. And for another group, it could be great leadership from extracurricular activities. In any case, you want to make sure that your resume highlights what *you've* specifically accomplished in a way that's relevant and compelling for the specific recruiting director reading it.

As it happens, Lisa's revamped resume worked pretty well with the recruiting directors she was targeting. "I attended the major league baseball job fair in New Orleans and got so many compliments on my resume," she e-mailed. "I ended up with ten interviews, five job offers, and a full-time position with the Los Angeles Dodgers at their AA affiliate in Jacksonville starting this summer!"

The message is that a well-written resume will stand out and get you noticed. But you need to put in the time and effort. Shoddy work just won't cut it.

Shocking Resume Confession #11
Fifty percent of resumes are bad or outright unreadable, and another 49 percent aren't as good as they could be.

Half the resumes I received as a recruiting director got tossed in the garbage in less than five seconds. They were so weak and so poorly written that I could tell right away they wouldn't make the cut. Then another 49 percent were like Lisa's—not necessarily awful, but certainly not as good as they could have been.

It's crazy when you think about it. Getting a job after college is extremely difficult, yet most people go into battle totally unprepared. You wouldn't take a final exam without studying, or write a paper without doing any research, would you? Or at least, if you did, you would know going in what the results were likely to be.

Getting a job is obviously much more difficult, and conceivably much more important, than any final or paper, yet students take it far too lightly.

One of the biggest problems students encounter is that they get bad advice from all sorts of people.

Nothing against your roommate, your older cousin, or your mom, but they probably aren't the best sources for putting together your resume. Yet time and time again, I hear the same refrain: "Well, my sister's boyfriend told me to put that on my resume."

Just because someone has a job doesn't mean that he or she is qualified to prepare resumes. Just because you cook a little doesn't qualify you to be a gourmet restaurant chef!

Think about it this way. Would you have your roommate, older cousin, or your mom cut your hair? Or fix your car? Or set a bone if you broke it?

I'm guessing not!

Make sure you get solid, qualified support. Start with your career center; if you'd like more help, seek out companies or services that are staffed by former recruiters. You want guidance from people who have actively read thousands of resumes and made hundreds of hiring decisions.

The reason most resumes aren't as good as they can be leads us to . . .

Shocking Resume Confession #12
Almost all students write job description resumes instead of accomplishment resumes.

Students simply describe what they did on their job, as opposed to telling the recruiting director what they actually accomplished.

We saw Lisa's resume, but now let's look at an example that could be a little closer to home. And by the way, I've seen this literally hundreds of times on resumes.

Waitress, Olive Garden, Pittsburgh, PA, Summer 2005

- Related to customers while taking orders, serving food and beverages, and bussing
- Delivered personalized customer service and conveyed knowledge of menu

Think about what is written for a second. Maybe at first glance it looks okay, but it's entirely generic and doesn't tell the reader anything they don't already know.

Allow me to let you in on a little secret. I've actually eaten at a restaurant before. In fact, it's safe to assume that all recruiting directors have eaten at restaurants. We know exactly what a waitress does! There is no benefit in simply explaining what ANY waitress has EVER done in the history of the restaurant business!

The same goes for sales associate, bank teller, construction worker, intern, club president, and so on. In fact, the recruiting director probably knows the general job description for any job, internship, or extracurricular activity on your resume.

What a typical recruiting director is dying to find out is:

- What YOU specifically accomplished
- What made YOUR experience unique
- What YOU AND ONLY YOU can put on the resume

If you held a "mundane" job like the ones listed above, think about what you did that was unique. Did you ever win Employee of the Month? Did you win a contest to sell the most pies or margaritas or whatever?

Were you the waitress who consistently generated the highest tip percentage? Did you work more than fifty hours a week full-time, or more than ten hours a week while going to school? If yes, then list these accomplishments on your resume like this:

Waitress, Olive Garden, Pittsburgh, PA, Summer 2005

- Awarded Employee of the Month in July for superior customer service
- Selected by management to cover more tables and more transactions than any other waitress
- Worked 55 hours a week to help finance college education

If not, don't list *anything* as a description for the job, but keep the job on your resume, without bullet points, to show that you did work over the summer and didn't just hang out by the pool.

Waitress, Olive Garden, Pittsburgh, PA, Summer 2005

But filling up your resume with obvious job descriptions is a complete waste of space.

Shocking Resume Confession #13
If what's written on your resume can also be written by the person who held that job or position before you, after you, or next to you, then you haven't done yourself justice.

This is the single best way to get your resume to stand out, and it is also the most difficult skill to master. Once you do it, though, your resume will be part of the small group of well-written resumes.

We saw in Lisa's resume how a resume full of accomplishments looks and how much recruiters love it. You'll find an appendix filled with great accomplishment resumes. Now let's talk about how you can do it.

When you're thinking about what to put under the descriptions of your jobs, internships, extracurriculars, and volunteer work in the experience section, you want to focus on two key areas: scope and results.

Scope—How big was the project you worked on?

1. How many numbers did you enter into the database?

2. How many press releases did you write?

3. How many people received the newsletter you edited?

4. How many computers were you responsible for in the lab?

5. How much inventory did you unload working on the dock?

6. How many people attended the event you planned on campus?

Results—What happened as a result of your actions?

1. What did they use the database for?

2. What publications picked up your press releases?

3. How many donations did you get from your newsletter?

4. Did you diminish the wait time for computer help at the lab?

5. Did the amount of inventory handled increase over the course of the summer?

6. Was it the largest campus event in your organization's history?

I cannot stress how important it is to fill your resume with accomplishments versus job descriptions. The problem that most students have is they think of their resume from their perspective and not from that of a recruiting director. In your mind, you know what you did. In your mind, you know how hard you worked. In your mind, you know what you've accomplished. But that does you absolutely no good if the reader of the resume doesn't know what you've done. And as we said before, recruiting directors are a cynical lot: they don't assume the best; they assume the worst.

Think back to Lisa's resume. Do statements like "responsible for all of the documents directed to project manager," "created progress spreadsheets," or "generated ticket sales for the Bears season in Champaign" mean anything to you? Not really. You have no idea what she did.

So recruiting directors end up not really knowing the extent of your experience. They don't really know if you're qualified for the job. As a result, your resume doesn't do nearly a good enough job in helping you get noticed. Let's look at some before and after examples and see what sounds better to you.

BEFORE	**AFTER**
Worked with businesses to carry out United Way fund-raising goals	Partnered with more than 20 area businesses to raise $15,000 for United Way, exceeding fund-raising goals by 23 percent
Helped accountants with various public accounting projects	Assisted accountants auditing $55,000 in accounts receivables for company's largest client
Developed marketing plans to promote concert series on campus	Developed fully integrated marketing campaign distributed to 10,000 students campuswide, resulting in 12 percent increase in concert attendance

It makes a pretty big difference, doesn't it? The appendix is filled with resumes that will show you how to write an accomplishment resume. You'll also notice one thing in common that all the "after" examples include.

Shocking Resume Confession #14
Great resumes are infused with facts, figures, and numbers.

If you don't have numbers on your resume, chances are it's just the same old job-description resume. Work hard to fill your resume with facts and figures.

Now for every entry on your resume, you're not going to necessarily have tons of numbers, but you'll be surprised at just how many you may have if you really think about it. Don't be afraid to go back to an organization or to an old boss and ask for help to fill in the blanks about what you did.

As a result of asking yourself the questions above, entries like . . .

- Entered numbers into a database

  Become . . .

- Entered more than 1,000 numbers into company's first business prospecting database, helping generate more than $2,000 in revenue

  And . . .

- Prepared competitive analysis

  Becomes . . .

- Prepared twelve-agency competitive analysis presented to client's upper management, resulting in $50,000 in additional spending

It makes a world of difference to the recruiting director to know exactly what you did and exactly why you're uniquely qualified for the job. If you want to land a job, fill your resume with numbers!

So there you have it. Fourteen shocking confessions about how a recruiting director looks at a resume. But wait, there's more! Recruiting directors are a tough bunch to please.

TEN RESUME MISTAKES THAT DRIVE RECRUITING DIRECTORS CRAZY

1. *Strict Chronological Resumes*

We already know that recruiting directors skim a resume in ten to fifteen seconds. Just like you'd skim an ad or a newspaper, they start at the top and work their way down. Obviously in that amount of time, they can't read everything on the resume.

As such, you certainly want to put the most important experiences first. Yet for some reason, many college grads have an obsession with making sure a resume is in chronological order. It just doesn't make sense.

If you worked as a waiter at Sweet Willie's Rib Shack in the summer of 2005, but as a financial analyst at Smith Barney in the summer of 2004, you should unquestionably put the Smith Barney job first under the experience section on your resume. There's a very good chance that the reader won't even make it to the Smith Barney job if the first thing the reader sees on your resume is the waiter job.

2. *Burying the Most Important Information*

As I stressed in the point above, we read a resume the same way we read an ad—top to bottom and left to right. So just like you should list your most important job first, you should also include the most important information *about* each job or entry first. For example, students will write:

Fall 2005, Alpha Tau Omega, Fraternity (President)

The recruiter may not even make it to the word *President*, which is of course the most important information. It should read:

President, Alpha Tau Omega, Fraternity, Fall 2005

Dates are the least important information; they should always go last. Either your title or where you worked should go first, depending on what is more impressive to the recruiter. Just make sure it's consistent throughout the resume. In this instance, not to knock the folks at Alpha Tau Omega, but the title, President, is more important, so that should go first.

In some instances the organizations or companies will go first throughout your resume if they are more impressive. Let's say you worked at Nike over the summer—but in the mailroom!

Nike Inc., Mailroom Assistant, Beaverton, OR, Summer 2005

Just remember the reader and what will be most impressive to him or her.

3. *The Skeeter McGee Honorary Scholarship*

Do you know what the Skeeter McGee Honorary Scholarship is? Neither do I. Yet time and again, students list entries like this on their resume. For all I know, the Skeeter McGee Honorary Scholarship is a full four-year tuition scholarship given to one student out of ten thousand applicants based on academics, leadership, and community service. Or Skeeter is your uncle, and he gave you one hundred dollars to buy beer when you turned twenty-one.

Keep thinking about your reader. Make sure the reader is familiar with what's listed on your resume, or he or she will assume it has no value. Remember, not every recruiter went to your school!

Here's how you should write about scholarships and awards. If it is a prominent honor, write it as:

Skeeter McGee Honorary Scholarship, full four-year tuition scholarship granted to one student out of 10,000 based on academics, leadership, and community service

Alternatively, if the Skeeter McGee is just some random scholarship that anyone on campus gets just because they have a 3.0 GPA, write it as:

Skeeter McGee Honorary Scholarship, awarded based on superior academics

I've worked with students who don't even know why they got an award or scholarship. If they have no idea what the award is, I promise you the recruiters won't know, and trust me, they're not going to "Google" it or call the school!

4. *Touting Your Computer Skills*

How many graduating college seniors do you think are familiar with Microsoft Word?

How many graduating college seniors list Microsoft Word on their resume?

Why? These days, it's a given that any new hire is going to know Word, PowerPoint, and Excel, or could learn them in a day. There's no need to list basic computer skills on your resume unless the job description asks for them. Of course advanced skills, those that are necessary for the job, should always be included.

Students sometimes say, "But I'll need to use Word every day at the office. Won't they want to know that I know it?" Well, you'll also have to use the telephone every day, and I sure hope you don't have "Ability to dial telephone" on your resume.

By the same token, forget about telling the recruiting director you know Internet Explorer. Is that supposed to impress me, or let me know you'll be spending quite a bit of time at work checking out the latest deals on eBay? Shockingly, about 10 percent of resumes still include the fact that the applicant knows how to use the Internet.

5. Vague (or Wrong) Objectives

If you're applying for a specific job at a specific company, then no, you don't need an objective. Obviously your objective is to get that job. While working at an ad agency, I can't tell you the number of times students put, "To obtain a position as a financial analyst at a commercial bank" as their objective and then accidentally sent that version of their resume to me.

More often than not, the objectives I received were fluffy space fillers like:

To use my outstanding communication, leadership, and analytical skills for a challenging position with diversity, travel, and room for growth in a large multinational corporation.

First of all, anyone can say that on a resume. Truly anyone can just *write* that they have outstanding communication skills or leadership skills or analytical skills, or any other self-ascribed attribute. A recruiting director wants to see proof of these skills as opposed to just lists of them. If she reads in the experience section of your resume that you gave more than thirty presentations on the dangers of drunk driving to local high school students, chances are you have outstanding communication skills. Secondly, you aren't telling the reader, who is only looking at your resume for fifteen seconds, anything unique by just listing random skills. In essence, an objective like the one above is just a waste of space and time.

If you want to work at a company and you're not sure if they have an opening, and you're not even sure who to send your resume to, you can have a very short and specific objective:

To obtain a position in the marketing department at Pepsi

This way the person who receives the resume knows which department or area to send it to. You should try to tailor your objective for specific companies and job titles if possible. If you're going to a career fair, or giving it to someone for general jobs, either keep an objective off completely or put something like:

To obtain a position in the marketing department of a consumer products company

6. *Gimmicks, Fancy Paper, and Cool Layouts*

There's a big difference between "good unique" and "bad unique" when it comes to resumes. Some people think the goal is to get their resume to stand out any way possible. I've received resumes laminated to look like four-page menus. I've gotten cardboard cutouts of resumes in the shape of a star. I've received polka dot resumes with streamers attached. I've even received pictures attached to a resume. Now, that's not impressive. That's just plain weird!

When you flip through a magazine, do you buy every product for every ad that stands out? Of course not. The same goes for a recruiter. What is going to make your resume be selected is not a gimmick; that only tells me you have no substance in the resume. What is going to make your resume stand out is compelling content, elegantly told. Save the cutouts for art class!

7. *Microscopic Font Size*

Oftentimes students think they can cram more information into a one-page resume by shrinking the font. Recruiting directors don't fall for that. And if they can't read your resume, chances are they're not going to pull out a magnifying glass to see it. Remember, recruiters are older than you and have weaker eyes.

8. *High School*

If you are a senior in college, nobody cares anymore about what you did in high school. I hate to tell you this, but the fact that you were treasurer of the National Honor Society as a sophomore in high school is no longer relevant.

If you had an internship or experience in high school that's extremely relevant to the job you're applying for, you can include it. Or if you accomplished something in high school that was an extraordinary national accomplishment, you can include it. Otherwise, your resume should just be about your college years.

If you're a junior, you can have high school information from your senior year. And as a sophomore or freshman in college, you'll have a lot more high school on your resume. Think of your resume as a rolling four-year history.

9. *Writing in the First Person and Using Complete Sentences*
On a resume, you're trying to convey as much relevant information as you can, as quickly as possible. Don't write in complete sentences, and don't use the words *I, me, we* or *our*. You should use a more objective style.

BAD	**GOOD**
I managed a team of eight other cooks in preparing the food for the restaurant	Managed a team of eight cooks preparing all restaurant food
Our team placed third at the national competition in San Francisco	Team placed third at national competition in San Francisco
I helped the Vice President of Finance fill out all of the tax forms for the 2005 season	Assisted Vice President of Finance with all 2005 tax forms

All of your student life, you're trying to stretch when you write: "I need to write a ten-page paper, and all I have is two pages of material."

In the real world, it's just the opposite. Recruiting directors don't like to read, so keep it short but compelling.

You should use bullet points underneath your education, experience, and activities/interests entries. Use action verbs to begin each bullet: past tense for experiences in the past, and present tense for jobs/activities you are currently involved with. Because you are using bullet points, there should be no periods on your resume.

10. Grammatical, Spelling, Diction Errors

You might as well just drop the resume in the garbage. There's simply no excuse for this! However, it's estimated that 15 percent of resumes contain at least one typo.

Believe it or not, I have received resumes that haven't even been spell-checked! And even spell-check doesn't catch everything. For instance, I once read a resume that said:

Responsible for ruining a team of eight full-time employees

I have a sneaking feeling he meant *running* a team!

Make sure you get at least two other people to proofread your resume. They will pick up mistakes that you didn't catch since you've read it so many times.

If recruiting directors get six hundred resumes for a job posting, and ninety of them have a typo in them, do you think they say, "Oh, that's okay. I'm sure this guy has a lot on his plate right now and didn't have time to proofread it accurately"?

I don't think so.

The resume is the basic building block of the job search; everything else is supported by your resume. As you can see, though, most students do not start with a strong foundation. The key to a great resume is to:

- Write of your accomplishments and not just a job description
- Fill your resume with facts, figures, and numbers
- Remember the perspective of the recruiting director reading it
- Format the document so it's easy to read and focuses on the most important information first

In the appendix, you'll find more than thirty examples of before and after resumes that highlight all of the points above. Read them carefully to help inspire your own resume.

Then, once you've crafted an amazing resume, you're in great shape to dive into the job search. The next phase is to get that resume into as many hands as possible by networking your way to a job.

Networking—Let Your Friends Get You a Job

Six Shocking Networking Confessions from the Recruiting Department

Imagine you've graduated from college and just moved to a brand-new city, let's say Chicago, to start your first job. After a few weeks it's time for that ever-important first haircut. What do you do?

Option 1: Try to research all five hundred hair salons in the city, carefully perusing the establishments for satisfied clients, typical clientele, number of stylists, and even salon owners' hair philosophies.

Option 2: Talk to your friend Kimberly, who is from Chicago, and say, "Hey, Kimberly, I really like your hair. Where do you get it cut?" and then try out that salon.

Chances are you're going to go with Option 2. It's a heck of a lot easier. You don't know for sure that her salon is the best in the city or even that you couldn't get a better haircut somewhere else. But you don't have the time nor do you want to go through the effort of checking them all out. Also, without a personal reference, you really don't know what you're ultimately going to get.

That's exactly how networking works when it comes to getting a job.

A recruiter has a huge stack of resumes to look through to find a candidate. But there are people at her company that will often know someone that they think would be a great new hire. The recruiter is almost always going to give serious consideration to those candidates that are recommended.

It's not to say that you're guaranteed a job if someone recommends you or that you won't get a job if you don't network. It's just that networking dramatically improves your chances of being hired.

If a recruiter has a stack of five hundred resumes to look through, there are typically about ten resumes on top of the pile that have been forwarded from someone inside the company. Chances are a recruiter will pick the best five of those ten off the top of the stack and then the best five of the remaining five hundred for an interview. The odds are a bit more in your favor!

Shocking Networking Confession #1
Roughly 64 percent of people get their jobs through networking and fewer than 4 percent get their jobs over the Internet.

So the question is, for every hour you spend on the Internet looking for a job, are you spending sixteen hours networking?

The answer is no, you are not. In spite of the fact that it is by far the best way to land a job, students avoid networking like the plague. There are two key reasons:

1. Students are afraid to network.

2. Students don't know how to network.

The thought of actually picking up the phone and calling a live person who works in the "real world" is petrifying. But let's try to put this daunting task into some context. Imagine you get a call one day at college and someone says, "Hi, my name is Murrel Fischer, and I'm a senior at Stevenson High School where you went to school. I see from our alumni database that you go to Haverford College and I was thinking about perhaps applying to the school. I was wondering if you would have thirty minutes to talk about what it's like to go to school there and how you got in?"

Would you say to him, "Who the hell do you think you are, calling me? Don't you know that I'm a college student? I don't have time for you!"

No, of course not. You would be delighted to talk to the kid from your school and probably be flattered that he even called you up. You'd give him all your perspective about what it's like to be a college student and probably even some tips about how to get into college.

That's exactly how it works in the real world.

Shocking Networking Confession #2
Most people you contact for networking will be dying to talk to you.

Here's why: People love to talk about themselves and give advice. Sounds funny, but it's true. So when they get a call from a nice young college student, they're excited to talk about how they "made it" and dispense all sorts of advice. Just think back to the high school student calling you. It's the same concept. Chances are, people in the real world won't think you're a nuisance, but rather, they will look forward to the chance to meet with you.

Now that you aren't afraid to contact someone, the other thing holding you back is that you don't know how to network—who to contact, what to say, how to follow up, and how to mention that you want a job. Let's get into it.

Shocking Networking Confession #3
You have way more contacts than you think.

The first step in networking your way to your first job is to collect names of people you can contact.

Whether you know it or not, your life is bursting with potential names. Just don't be shy when it comes to making contacts. Here's a list of some places to start:

- Your college career center—they typically have names of alums who have volunteered to talk to students
- Alums from any organizations you're a part of (sports teams, Greek life, business organizations, religious groups, volunteering)
- Your parents' friends
- Your friends' parents
- Your professors
- Doctors, dentists, and other professionals you know
- Basically anyone you interact with

You don't want to be shy about spreading the word that you're in the job hunt and you're looking for people to talk to. It's as simple as saying to your parents, "Hey, I'm considering a career in consulting when I graduate. Do you know if any of your friends work in consulting, or do you know if some of their friends might?" It's like the old "six degrees of separation" rule. If you are dying to work at Disney, you might not know anyone who works there, but chances are you know someone who knows someone who works at Disney. You need to find that person! Talk to all of your contacts, trying to get names at companies you're interested in, or even of people in the fields you'd like to work in.

Importantly, the names you capture don't have to be of the president or the recruiting director. They can literally be names of anyone at the company, just someone you can begin to talk with about the organization.

Once you have the names, you want to put together a spreadsheet to keep track of your contacts. Every successful project in life begins with a spreadsheet!

Take the names of your contacts and put them across the top. Then down the side list things like how you know them, their e-mail, phone, address, company, and job title, and any other relevant info. Then include a section to keep track of your communications with them. It can look something like this:

NAME:

NAME:

NAME:

NAME:

Relationship

Contact Info

Company

Title

First Call

Second Call

Third Call

You should aim to have at least twenty-five names on that list within three weeks of starting the process.

Next you want to get in touch with your contacts. Start with a phone call; it's always best to talk in person. Here's a sample of what to say:

"Hi, Mr. Peterson. My name is Tracy Marhula, and I received your name from a family friend of mine, David Michaels, who suggested I get in touch with you. I'm looking to get into consulting when I graduate this spring from the University of North Dakota and was hoping to learn a bit more about the field. I'm sure you're really busy, but I was wondering if it would be possible to meet for about twenty minutes at your convenience to ask you a few questions about you and your job at Accenture."

That wasn't so bad, was it? Try to get in touch with them in person. It's okay to call and hang up if you get their voice mail (you likely will), but remember, lots of people have caller ID, so don't call eight times a day! Once a day is enough. If you don't get through after a couple of days, leave a voice mail. Make it succinct, like the example above, and don't forget to leave your name and number.

If you don't hear back in about a week, send them an e-mail or call again. Make sure the subject line includes your connection to them: "Student from North Dakota looking for job advice" or "Referred by David Michaels." The e-mail should essentially be a written version of the script above.

Be realistic. There will be some people who don't call you back, never respond to the e-mail, or simply say no. So be it. That's not so bad. Fortunately many people will be happy to meet with you, even if it's not right away.

When you do make the contacts, it's time to schedule an informational interview.

Shocking Networking Confession #4
The biggest mistake that students make is coming into an informational interview and just waiting for questions to be asked.

An informational interview is a brief (twenty to thirty minute) meeting where you meet a professional in the field to learn more about the industry, the company, and that individual's career. You'll get to do most of the question asking, but you'll need to be prepared for them to ask you a few questions as well. It's usually a pretty low-stress, informative way to learn more about a career and get your foot in the door at a company.

Don't think that you're there just to answer a bunch of questions though. The entire basis for the meeting is that you want to find out more about the job, industry, career path, and so on. Come armed with at least fifteen questions that you're generally interested in discovering the answers to. They can be career-related questions like:

- How did you become interested in the field?
- How did you get your job here?
- What do you like about this job?
- What is the most difficult thing about this industry?
- What attracted you to the industry?
- What makes someone successful here?
- Describe a typical career path.
- What skills do you find yourself using consistently?
- What type of background do you think is important for this field?
- What technology skills are critical for new employees?

They can also be business-related questions relevant to the field like:

- How has the industry changed over the last ten years?
- How has consolidation affected the business?
- Where do you see the industry going in the next five years?
- What are the key business issues your company is facing?
- How do you differentiate your business from that of your competitors?

You want to show that you are curious, have done some homework on the field and company, and seem genuinely interested in learning more. You should also be prepared in case they do ask you some questions, but don't plan on that being the entire focus of the meeting.

While the overt intent isn't to be asking for a job on these interviews, of course you're going to be leaving an impression with this person. You want to make sure you look as buttoned up as can be.

Shocking Networking Confession #5
You need to treat an informational interview with as much professionalism as a real interview.

Oftentimes students will think, "Cool, it's an informational interview. I can wear jeans and just chill as this dude tells me what it's like to be a professional." Sorry, that's not how it works. The only difference between an informational interview and a job interview is that you need to do the asking and not wait around for someone to throw questions at you.

Here's what to do:

- Dress professionally—business suit, even if the company is casual
- Show up on time—at least five to ten minutes early
- Bring extra copies of your resume
- Be respectful of their time—if you set the appointment up for twenty minutes, be sure to check with them if the meeting is running longer
- Politely ask for more networking names—this keeps your networking pipeline full
- Ask them if it's okay to leave a copy of your resume—this way you'll be top-of-mind if they do have an opening

Here's a perfect end to the fictitious meeting you had with Mr. Peterson of Accenture:

> "Tracy, it was great meeting with you today. I hope I answered some of your questions about consulting and Accenture. If you have an extra copy of your resume, I'd love to forward it to our recruiting department in case we have any openings. Also, here are the names of a few more people you may want to talk to at other consulting firms."

Again, even though it's not a traditional "interview," it's your chance to make a favorable impression with a potential employer. You want Mr. Peterson to forward your resume to HR with a little note that says, "Hey, I just met this great candidate named Tracy Marhula, and next time we have an opening, I think you should interview her."

And just like in our hair salon story at the beginning, when it comes time for that recruiting director to hire someone, your resume will be at the top of the list with special consideration to be interviewed.

Don't think the networking process ends after the interview.

Shocking Networking Confession #6
Your ability to stay top-of-mind with your networking contact is critical to landing a job.

The informational interview is only the start. Immediately after you meet, send a nice thank-you note, either handwritten or e-mailed. Make sure to make it personal and reference what you talked about in the interview (see Chapter 5 on thank-you notes for more detail).

Then, continue the dialog. After about a month, either call or e-mail with the latest on your job search. Try something like, "I wanted to let you know that I met with Darin Johns per your suggestion and he gave me even more information about consulting. I am now more convinced than ever that I would love a career in the field." If your contact responds, then continue e-mailing or calling. This keeps you top-of-mind for when a position may come up. You should also let them know when you do land a job, even if it's not at their company. Remember, networking doesn't just end when you get the job; it's something to do for a lifetime.

When it comes to landing work, the old adage, "It's not what you know, it's who you know," couldn't be truer. Your potential to "know" a lot of people is out there just waiting to be tapped. Don't be shy about getting names. Don't be shy about calling people up. And don't be shy about staying in contact. Remember, you have basically a two-thirds chance of getting your job through networking, so you better take advantage of it.

Once you've written the great resume and gotten it into the hands of enough people through networking, then the informational interviews will turn into job leads. Soon thereafter you'll be asked to send your resume on to HR, and the recruiting directors in HR are going to ask for a cover letter to accompany that resume—the subject of our next chapter.

THREE

Cover Letters— The "Teaser" for Your Resume

Ten Shocking Confessions to Help You Write a Great Cover Letter

I know exactly what your cover letter says, yet I can assure you I'm not a mind reader. Let me guess. It's a single-spaced, full-page, four-paragraph letter, organized as follows:

Paragraph 1: How you heard about the job

Paragraph 2: Why you want the job

Paragraph 3: Why you'd be good at the job

Paragraph 4: How you intend to follow up about the job

In addition, you've taken what's already on your resume and simply rewritten it in paragraph form.

How do I know this? Because virtually every single college student writes *exactly the same* cover letter. It's amazing!

Shocking Cover-Letter Confession #1
Most cover letters are never read.

We already talked about the fact that recruiting directors get so many resumes that they barely spend fifteen seconds reading them. Do you really think they are going to spend an additional two minutes reading a longer version of your resume? I think not. But just because they aren't read doesn't mean you don't need one.

Shocking Cover-Letter Confession #2
You should never send out a resume without a cover letter.

I equate cover letters, the way they are currently being written, to a pharmaceutical ad you'd see in a magazine. Have you ever read the full page of legal text accompanying an ad for a drug? I doubt it. Yet every pharmaceutical advertisement must include that copy. Sadly, recruiting directors look at most cover letters and assume they are equally as boring. Yet most companies insist that you include a cover letter.

So why do companies ask for a cover letter? There are two reasons. One, they want to insure that you put in some extra effort to apply for their jobs. Simply sending your resume is far too easy, so some companies use it as a screen against people who apply to every job opening they ever see. Secondly, they are offering students a chance to show something more than just what's written on the resume. Alas, most students blow their big chance.

Shocking Cover-Letter Confession #3
Cover letters represent one of the best ways for students to set themselves apart.

Even though most of them do not get read, cover letters, when written well, are incredibly important. A cover letter is the very first piece of communication that an employer will see, even before the resume. It's the very first chance for you to make a favorable impression. And it's the very first way for you to emerge from the pack of candidates.

Students absolutely treat cover letters in the wrong way. Most of them simply write one cover letter and just reuse it over and over again, changing the name of the company each time it's sent out (and some students even forget to change the name!). Students also think they have to tell all, or most, of their life stories in the cover letters. That's why they don't get read.

Here's a typical cover letter. Looks familiar, doesn't it!

To whom it may concern:

I'm writing to express my interest in obtaining employment opportunities within your organization. Specifically I am interested in the home-merchandising position. Currently I am a senior at Montana State University and will be graduating in May of 2006 with a degree in textiles and clothing.

I think you will find that my background makes me very suited for a job at your company. During college, I have had the opportunity to learn and grow into myself. As you can see from my attached resume, I have been able to supplement my textiles-and-clothing curriculum with many business classes and activities. The additional courses have given me more confidence with my education and rounded out my knowledge of the fashion industry with both style and business. I was able to pursue studies in classes covering home merchandising, store merchandising, design, production, manufacturing, and a host of other topics. In addition I held an internship at Spiegel and worked in St. Louis in the buying department of the May Company. Finally, I was involved in helping to put together a fashion show on campus.

Your company strives for quality in both customer service and fashion, and those qualities have encouraged me to seek a position. During my education and work experience, I have gained knowledge in both business and in fashion. With these skills, I feel that I would be an asset to your team. Through my desire to grow and my need for challenge, both your company and I could benefit greatly by including me on your team.

I look forward to the opportunity to interview with you. I very much would like to work with your organization and feel as though I would be a valuable contributor. Please expect a call from me to confirm specific details around an interview.

Sincerely,

Susan Sullivan

When you really read it closely, this cover letter says very little, and certainly doesn't do a very good job in selling the candidate. Every single thing she mentions is perfectly apparent by looking at her resume. Now imagine getting about four hundred of these letters a week. No wonder recruiting directors don't read most cover letters!

Think of your cover letter in an entirely different way. Think of your cover letter as a "teaser" for your resume. You know what teaser ads are: those commercials on TV or in a magazine where they don't tell you everything about a product, but instead just pique your curiosity or interest. You want to do the same thing for your resume. Write enough—just enough—to get the recruiting director interested in spending more time with your resume.

So what do you write? Unlike every other student in America, please do not just take what's already written on your resume and rewrite it! Do something totally different. Make the cover letter personal. Tell some type of story about you that's not apparent from your resume—something that's different, special, or unique about you. But remember, there's a fine line between clever . . . and stupid!

Shocking Cover-Letter Confession #4
Cover letters need to be unique, personal, and attention getting.

This is how you invite the recruiting director in and actually get her to read your cover letter. She has no interest in simply reading your resume in paragraph form. By writing an interesting cover letter, you're taking the first important step to sell yourself.

The other critical factor in putting together your cover letter is length. There is no need to drone on and on about everything you've ever done in your entire life or to fill up a full single-spaced page. Folks, you're not writing a term paper. Longer isn't better! As we mentioned in the resume chapter, people in the working world don't have a lot of time on their hands and don't want to read too much. Keep it short, interesting, and inviting.

Shocking Cover-Letter Confession #5
When it comes to cover letters, shorter is better.

You should write a cover letter that's ten sentences long (give or take). Your paragraphs should be short, and your sentences should be short. Again, it's not a college paper, which you must stretch out. Be direct. Get right to the point. And make the first line a killer!

Try to talk about how you became interested in the field, or in the company, and tell a story about why you'd make a great candidate.

Here's an example:

Dear Ms. Smith,

Dog food.

Yes, dog food got me hooked on advertising.

My sophomore year in college I took a class where we had to create a fully integrated campaign for Purina Dog Chow. Everything about the project intrigued me—the teamwork, the creativity, the strategy, but most of all the fact that every facet of every class every day was different.

From that point it was all over.

I knew I had to work in advertising and spent the remainder of my college days pursuing that dream. Whether it was as president of our Ad Club, an intern at Tilbury Advertising, or as an account executive on our National Student Advertising Competition Team, my passion for the field intensified.

I'm now anxious to parlay my experiences into a full-time job at DDB Advertising—a company I know is dedicated to creating amazing work.

I'll plan to follow up in a week's time. In the meantime, feel free to contact me.

Regards,

Jennifer Andersen

Not your typical cover letter, eh? But here's the thing. These are the types of cover letters that recruiting directors crave. They are much more interesting to read than the same full-page garbage that simply repeats what is already written on your resume. This letter is interesting, it's easy to read, and most importantly it tells recruiting directors something unique about you that isn't apparent from your resume.

Cover letters also offer the opportunity to tell the recruiting director something you'd like them to know about you or your resume that might not make sense upon first glance. Maybe you have a story about why you'd be a perfect fit for the company, or why someone with your background is pursuing a job in that field, or why you bring some special skill or unique fit to the organization.

Shocking Cover-Letter Confession #6
Cover letters can help make a company consider you when you might normally be rejected.

Check this one out:

Dear Ms. Pike:

Why would a biology major want to work in finance?

That's a great question, and one I've asked myself on several occasions. At first glance it seems like a disconnect, but upon reflection, it actually makes quite a bit of sense.

Finance and biology share much in common. Finance is all about creating something (wealth) by using a variety of tested but ultimately unproven techniques. Very little in finance is definite. Even though a fund or a stock is performing well now, there's no sure way to know how it will do in the future.

Biology is pretty similar. It's also about knowing the background, studying the conditions, and making educated guesses about what will happen in the future. It's rooted in research and facts and knowledge.

My interest in finance doesn't just come from the biology lab. It also comes from a host of activities outside the classroom. I started our university's first finance association, managing a collective portfolio that earned a 23 percent rate of return. I've also had two great finance internships.

I hope to get the chance to talk to you more about how a biology major can make a difference at Morgan Stanley. I'll plan to follow up with you in a week's time.

Regards,

Jack Landsberg

This letter is a bit longer than the first, but the way it's written makes it an easy read. How can you possibly look at that first sentence and not want to keep reading? It also takes a negative (unrelated major) and turns it into a positive. Wouldn't you want to interview Jack?

What you say in your cover letter depends quite a bit on the field that you're going into and the specific jobs you are applying for.

Shocking Cover-Letter Confession #7
Just like a resume, your cover letter needs to be targeted to your employer.

If you are applying in a field that's more creative, you can have more fun with your cover letter. When you send a cover letter to more conservative companies, then you need to tone it down a bit. But remember, conservative doesn't mean boring. Jack's letter above is for a finance job, one of the more reserved fields, but it still works.

Typically you can get away with one version of your cover letter per field. In other words, if you're applying for jobs within the same general area, you can write one version and then simply change the company names and make any other minor modifications.

But you should have different cover letters for each field. You'd want a different cover letter for a consulting job versus a job in engineering. And again, based on your "story" for each of these fields, the letter will be totally different.

For writing jobs—journalism, public relations, publishing—you absolutely MUST write a great cover letter. Would you hire someone for a writing job who didn't compose a unique, interesting cover letter? Yet time and again, students simply send out the same old boring regurgitated cover letter for these positions. Your cover letter is in essence your writing sample, and it plays a huge role in getting you the job. Take extra time and effort to make it great.

So what exactly do you say in a great cover letter? We saw a couple of examples above, but obviously your story needs to be unique to you. (Don't just copy the cover letters!).

Shocking Cover-Letter Confession #8
Every cover letter needs to have a story.

The story can make or break your cover letter. Also critical is how you attract someone with the first line. We talked above about how recruiting directors don't read most cover letters. If you can pull them in with a great introductory sentence, they're more apt to read your entire cover letter. It's just like any ad you may read in a magazine or newspaper. If you're not engaged by reading the first line, chances are you won't read any further.

Here are some topics to consider when crafting your story and some ways to think about the first line. Remember two things. First, it has to be YOUR story, something you can discuss intelligently in an interview. And second, there's a fine line between clever and stupid, so be careful!

- How you became attracted to the field:

  I've been interested in finance since my dad introduced me to the stock tables when I was thirteen years old.

- Some interesting experience related to the field:

You wouldn't think that a college junior would be solely responsible for planning a fashion show attended by 300 people.

- A great opportunity that you had:

Most student interns don't get the chance to travel to Singapore on a business trip.

- An extensive background in the field:

Believe it or not, I've been involved in consulting since I was eleven years old.

- A strong passion for the job responsibilities:

I'm the kind of person that lives for deadlines, pressure, and change.

Ask yourself why you're interested in the field, in the job, in the company. Ask yourself why you'd do well there. Ask yourself what makes you a unique or special candidate. These questions all provide the inspiration for the story of your cover letter.

Check out the appendix for several examples of great cover letters highlighting the categories above.

Sometimes you don't even need a story to write an impactful cover letter. In some instances a personal connection can do the trick!

Shocking Cover-Letter Confession #9
Don't be shy about dropping a name in your cover letter.

Maybe you're one of the lucky ones. Maybe your mom plays golf with the president of the company you're dying to work at, or maybe your brother knows someone who works in the HR department of Dream Job, Inc. Heck, your dentist might know some guy who works in information technology for a fabulous organization.

In the networking chapter, we talked about how you need to use your connections to get your foot in the door for an informational interview. The ideal outcome for one of those interviews is that your connection forwards your resume to the recruiting director with a little note mentioning how great you are. Alternatively, after the informational interview, the person you know may say, "Why don't you send your resume on to HR and mention that you and I met." You can't always expect them to do all the work for you!

In this case, don't be shy about dropping the name.

Shocking Cover-Letter Confession #10
Mention your company connection in the first line of the cover letter.

If you've got it, flaunt it! There's no reason to hold back on what is most likely to be your best shot to get an interview. You definitely still want to tell your cover-letter story, but now it will have even more impact given the connection. Here's an example:

Dear Mr. Pellettieri:

Eric Patt, from your event management department, and I met the other day and he suggested I contact you. He and I had a great conversation about the intricacies of pulling off the annual Paul Palmer event and all the planning and details that go into such a huge undertaking.

The more we talked, the more I recognized the similarities between a job at Windy City Fieldhouse and my event-planning experiences at school. I was selected as the only student on campus to help plan our 150th anniversary celebration.

It was an unbelievable experience. I don't think I ever worked harder at anything else in my life, but I loved every second of it. The planning and the execution certainly had some ups and downs, but in the end it was a spectacular event, and I can't tell you how gratifying it felt to know that I played a part in the success.

I'm extremely anxious to share my passion, my dedication, and my experience with a company like yours. Based on what Eric told me, I know I'd be able to make a contribution to Windy City Fieldhouse right away.

I look forward to touching base soon. I'll plan to follow up in a week's time.

Regards,

David Wilkov

Don't feel like your connection has to be some senior manager or the CEO of the company in order to make it work. Someone, *anyone,* will help you get noticed. At my former job, referrals from well-performing middle managers or junior staff actually held more promise for me since I figured these folks really knew the quality and the caliber of whom they were referring. Oftentimes the CEO types were merely passing on the name of the son of their investment club associate or bridge partner whom they had never even met before.

Of course there may be rare instances when dropping a name isn't the best idea. For instance, if you're talking with your older brother's college buddy who works at your dream company and he says something like, "This company is okay, but they have a really strict policy on stealing office supplies. I mean I tried to take a dozen staplers home the other day, and now I'm on probation for six months," you may not want to associate yourself with klepto boy!

Whether or not you have a company connection, your cover letter can be an amazing tool to help you get the job. There were times when I interviewed someone who had a great, attention-getting, clever cover letter but a lousy resume. It's a chance for you to tell your story, to make a personal connection, and to get someone interested in you beyond what they already see in your resume. Of course it takes time and effort to craft a great cover letter, but it's an investment that is sure to pay off.

With a great cover letter to capture their attention, and with a wonderful resume that highlights your accomplishments, you're bound to get that call from a recruiting director to come in for an interview. Now the fun stuff starts! Read on to learn how to ace the job interview.

FOUR

Interviewing—
You Never Get a Second Chance
to Make a First Impression

Eighteen Shocking Confessions You Better Know Before You Interview

You did it. You actually convinced someone to interview you. Your resume passed the fifteen-second test, and you were selected from a huge pool of applicants for an interview.

Here's your prize. You get the pleasure of sitting across from someone who, for about thirty minutes, can and will grill you on ANYTHING about your past, present, or future. You'll be wearing an uncomfortable business suit, trying to act perfectly formal and proper. And you'll be attempting to sound like an aspiring businessperson as opposed to a normal college student whose primary concern is avoiding 9:00 a.m. classes for an entire semester.

Oh, and your entire future rests on this thirty-minute interview.

Just past this interview, you can see the light at the end of the tunnel. The dream job is just sitting out there for the taking, and the only person standing in the way is the dastardly recruiting director, the person whose job it is to make sure you screw up the interview and you don't get the job.

You have it all wrong though.

Shocking Interview Confession #1
Recruiting directors actually want you to do well.

In spite of what you may be thinking, recruiting directors are not vengeful, spiteful, evil human beings placed on the earth for the sole purpose of deceiving, terrorizing, and tricking college students into ruining their one and only chance to get a job.

In fact, they are regular folks looking to make a connection in order to meet and hire great people. Yet for some reason, the legend of the evil recruiting director persists. Let's think about it for a second. My title at my former company was recruiting director. My job was to recruit people—in other words, to hire people for the company.

I would NOT come back from a university recruiting trip and say, "Guess what, boss? I was so evil, so terrorizing, so deceitful that I got each and every student to screw up during the interview and we're not hiring *anyone*!"

And he would NOT say, "Great job, Brad! You haven't hired anyone in five years. Keep up the good work; you're the best recruiting director we've ever had!"

The truth is, I would sit down before every single interview and think, "I really hope I like this candidate." There's nothing more gratifying than meeting someone who would make a wonderful addition to the company. Yet most of the students I interviewed thought they were standing trial and I was the judge, jury, and executioner.

Shocking Interview Confession #2
An interview should be approached as a
conversation with a friend.

Students think they need to take on a new interviewing persona to appeal to the working world. They tend to be way too stiff, formal, and unnatural. The best interviews are honest, interesting, and insightful conversations between two people. Now, this shouldn't be a conversation like, "Yo, dog, what's goin' down tonight? Are we gonna go out and rip it up or what?" But instead, think of it as a conversation that you might have with one of your friend's parents.

Most students, though, go into the interview thinking it's a battle of wits against someone who is out to defeat them.

So when you get a question like "Why did you decide to become an engineering major, Paul?" your mind probably operates like this:

The interviewer just asked me why I decided to become an engineering major. What I would normally say is that as far back as I can remember, I've always been fascinated by how things work, but what she probably means by asking that question is why do I think I'd be a great engineer, but she could also be really trying to find out why I think I'd be better than anyone else as an engineer, so maybe I should answer by saying that the reason I chose to be an engineer is that I'm confident I can be the best in my field, but that may sound overconfident, so maybe I should just say engineering is the sum total of all that works in the world and the best people that do it are the ones that have the best chance of succeeding in the real world and ultimately I want to succeed in the world and work for a great company like GE and one day aspire to be able to blah, blah, blah . . .

That's how good interviews go bad. Allow me to let you in on a little secret. The reason the recruiter asked you why you decided to become an engineering major is that she is legitimately interested in hearing why you decided to become an engineering major!

The recruiting director does not typically have a hidden agenda. There are no "secret questions" or specific answers that recruiters are looking to hear. They genuinely want a chance to get to know who you are and to find out what makes you tick.

But many students go through the following thought process every time a question is asked:

- Here's what she asked . . .
- Here's how I might answer the question . . .
- But here's what she probably means by the question . . .
- Here's what she probably wants me to answer . . .
- So here's what I should say.

And all that is going on in your brain every time a question is being asked. No wonder you hate interviewing!

The best advice is to be honest, interesting, and insightful. Again, think of the interview more as a discussion you might have with one of your professors as opposed to a formal police interrogation. Sit back, relax, and enjoy.

I know that advice sounds incredibly simple, but in actuality it is quite a bit more difficult. The best way to make an interview conversational and to feel comfortable is to practice.

Shocking Interview Confession #3
You should have a minimum of five mock interviews before your first "real" interview.

Think about the first paper you wrote in college versus one you wrote recently. Think about how you did on the first test you took versus how you do now. With everything in life, practice makes perfect.

You should NEVER walk into your first real interview without having practiced. The more often you put on the business suit, sit down, and talk about your accomplishments, the more comfortable you'll feel in an actual interview.

Practice with your career center, practice with professional job preparation companies, practice with your friends or with your parents, but make sure you practice! Even when you're mock interviewing with someone you know, you'll feel nervous, and this experience will help prepare you for an actual interview.

It's okay to feel a bit nervous when you interview. Everyone does, even veteran interviewees. In fact, the nervousness gives you a bit of an adrenaline rush that helps you stay on top of your game. And don't worry about looking nervous either. In actuality, you look much less nervous than you probably are. Students get nervous about being nervous and it adds to the pain. But you literally have to be visibly shaking for someone to tell that you're nervous.

Being nervous also comes from the "formality" of an interview. Let's be honest, an interview is not the most natural of situations. Oftentimes, though, students make the interviewing situation out to be much more proper than it needs to be.

Take your name for example. Students think that once they graduate college they have to go by their given, formal name in the "real world." So on the top of their resume, a guy named Steve Pereira will write:

Stephen Gomes Pereira III

Now Steve has gone by Steve his whole life. His friends call him Steve, and his classmates call him Steve, and his professors call him Steve. In fact, the only people to call him Stephen are his parents. And when do they do this? When he's in trouble. As in "Stephen Pereira, you get your sister off the chandelier this instant, or you won't see the light of day for a month!"

But Steve feels that now that he's an "adult," he should go by Stephen, or at least list his name as Stephen on his resume so that companies will be impressed by how "adult" he is. So Steve is sitting in the lobby at his dream company waiting to be interviewed and out walks the interviewer to greet him. The interviewer calls out, "Stephen Pereira." And subconsciously Steve thinks, "Damn, what did I do wrong?" because of course the only people who refer to him as Stephen are his parents when he's in trouble.

Now this may indeed be subconscious or it may not be. The result, though, is that you go into the interview on the defensive, thinking you've already done something wrong, and the person interviewing you suddenly assumes an even bigger position of authority and superiority.

Shocking Interview Confession #4
People named Steve, Cathy, Matt, and Jen will actually be hired by companies.

Recruiters don't say, "Good god, this candidate had the audacity to list her name as Cathy instead of Catherine. She'll never be Microsoft material." Trust me, they don't give it a second thought, but you feel awkward during the interview because you keep being referred to by a name you never use.

For heaven's sake, look at Bill Clinton and Jimmy Carter. They both made it to president of the United States without going by William and James. The message is don't make the interview even more formal and unnatural than it has to be by using a formal name that isn't what you normally go by.

That being said, if you went by "Stinky" in college, I don't think I'd put that on your resume.

So once you've had a few mock interviews under your belt, and listed your more familiar name, you will hopefully feel relaxed entering the interview process. Now, how do you best prepare?

Shocking Interview Confession #5
You can flunk an interview before it even starts by not researching the company and the job.

It sounds like basic information, but you'd be amazed at how many people are poorly prepared for interviews. I interviewed students who would ask me questions at the end of the interview like:

- What job am I interviewing for?
- Who is your company president?
- What clients do you have?
- Where are you located?

Guess what happened to these candidates? Most of them are now flipping burgers for a living! It's amazing, but many people don't take the time to prepare for interviews. Obviously, before you go on any interview, you should spend some time on the company's Web site, visit your career center at school, read "trade" publications specific to your field—industry journals like *AdAge* for advertising and *Variety* for entertainment—talk with your professors, and try to contact alumni or friends that may know someone at the company.

Now, you don't have to walk in to the interview quoting stock prices from the 1960s, but you should know a good deal about the organization.

A lot more important is what is called "you prep." The first part of "you prep" is knowing what the company is looking for and knowing what you've done. Sounds rather simplistic, but most people don't do it. Knowing what the company is looking for is pretty easy.

Shocking Interview Confession #6
A company's job description will usually tell you exactly the types of questions you'll be asked on an interview.

If the job description says something like "We are looking for creative problem solvers," you are almost guaranteed to get a question like "Give me an example of when you creatively solved a problem." Obviously that question is a lot easier to answer if you've thought about it in advance. And that's the key to a great interview—making sure you're not caught off guard and unprepared to answer. To be sure, there will be times when you are asked a question that you haven't thought about yet. A bit later we'll talk about how to deal with that situation. But for the most part, there shouldn't be too many times when you are asked something out of the blue.

When you check out the job description, simply think of a few examples for each of the traits the company lists for their ideal candidate. These examples can be from school, internships, jobs, extracurriculars, or really anything in life. Just make sure you can discuss a situation intelligently. If asked for an example of leadership, for instance, don't just say, "Yeah, I'm a leader," but instead talk about when you were a leader, what you learned, and how you think you can improve upon your leadership skills in the future.

Having these examples at your fingertips is important, but make sure you don't go overboard.

Shocking Interview Confession #7
Preparing for an interview does not mean memorizing a script.

You can go too far and sound too rehearsed and polished during an interview. This can be a big turnoff to companies. Simply be prepared to talk naturally about what you've accomplished and you'll do fine. You want to have specific examples at your fingertips, not a prerehearsed response that you've memorized.

The second part of "you prep" is knowing your strengths and weaknesses. Let's be honest. "What are your weaknesses?" could rank up there as the absolute most difficult interview question ever asked. I must admit, I did ask it on occasion, and here are some of the responses I would get:

Twenty percent of the time—"Hmmm . . . uh . . . (*student begins to blush*) . . . uh . . . let me think . . . (*student begins to sweat*) . . . uh . . . uh . . . I know there's something . . . (*student begins to blush and sweat at the same time*) . . . uh . . . I just can't think of anything right now."

That's arguably the worst possible way to answer any question. Those people never got the job.

Seventy-five percent of the time—"Actually, Brad, my weakness is I work too hard, and I tend to be a perfectionist."

That's arguably the biggest bull @#$% answer in the history of interviewing.

I know what the student is thinking: "I'm going to take a strength and *disguise* it as a weakness, and this recruiting director here, who interviews people for a living, will never figure that trick out!" Guess what? You're not the first person to pull that stunt.

Shocking Interview Confession #8
Recruiting directors are not idiots. They know the old take-a-strength-and-disguise-it-as-a-weakness trick.

It's really quite pathetic. By trying to pull the strength-to-weakness stunt, you basically tell the recruiting director that you're looking for the easy way out and that you aren't an independent thinker or capable of being introspective—not necessarily the best things to be conveying on an interview.

The remaining five percent of the students answered the weakness question properly. They actually took a real weakness and talked about it in a compelling and insightful way.

That's exactly how you want to handle the weakness question. Think about the following:

- What your weakness is
- How you discovered it
- Why it's important to fix it
- How you're trying to improve upon it

So, when someone asks what your weakness is, you can say something like:

"One of the things I'm working on right now is my tendency to procrastinate. I know once I start working full-time I won't have the luxury of putting things off until the last minute. Right now when I procrastinate, it really only affects me. I might get a lower grade than I wanted on a paper or test. But in the "real world" I'll be working in teams and I know I won't be able to let the rest of the group down.

I realized that now, when I do a project, I tend to wait until the last minute to do the things I don't really like doing. So, every day, I write down a to-do list and make sure the first things I do are the ones I don't want to. I even made a bet with my roommate that I'd get those done first. If I don't, I have to buy him lunch, and trust me, I don't want to do that! I'm not perfect at it yet, but I'm getting a lot better."

That sounds better than "You know what, I'm a perfectionist. I'm *too* good at what I do."

It works for pretty much any weakness you have, unless it's something like "I just don't like to be around people. I tend to get violent." But seriously, avoid what we call "red flag" weaknesses like "I don't like numbers" for a finance job, or "I hate details" for an administrative job. But in most cases, a well-thought-out weakness can make you sound quite impressive.

Shocking Interview Confession #9
Recruiting directors are typically less interested in what your actual weakness (or strength) is and more interested in how you discuss it.

Again, assuming it's not a hideous weakness, talking about something with insight, with reflection, and with an eye to the future says a lot about who you are and how you think.

Strengths are quite a bit easier, since you don't have to say that you're bad at something. But think about it the same way. Why are you strong at something and how does it relate to the job? If you have a lot of strengths (and of course you do), try to pick just a couple that you think would be most relevant to your success at the company you're interviewing with.

> *"I think one of my strongest areas is my ability to multitask. I've always been involved in quite a few things, and I really enjoy the rush of having a lot going on. I actually found out that I do better in school when I'm more active outside the classroom. For instance, right now I'm taking a full course load and double majoring in marketing and finance. I'm very involved in student government as vice president of the senior class. I'm also on the school's rugby team, which includes daily practices and weekend games, and I've even found time to volunteer once a week at the local middle school."*

Once you've done the job prep and done the "you prep," you're ready for the meat of the interview. Most companies conduct behavioral interviews. It's really a pretty simple concept. It just means that they are interested in how you've behaved in previous situations in life, figuring that how you've acted in the past will predict how you'll act in the future.

Shocking Interview Confession #10
Interviewers are far more interested in your "whys" and your "hows" than your "whats."

The "whats" are what got you the interview. Those are the listings on your resume like your school, your grades, your jobs, and your activities.

Now recruiters want to know what drives your behavior and why you did the things you did.

For instance, I used to start every interview with the same basic question. "Oh, I see that you went to the University of North Carolina. Why did you decide to go there?" (Of course I would only ask this question of them if they actually went to the University of North Carolina . . . but you knew that).

The range of responses that I got from that simple question was amazing. Some students would say:

"Actually, when it came time to select a college, I wanted to go to a large school, since I went to a very small high school. Diversity of the student body, a strong academic reputation, great involvement opportunities, and big-time college sports were all important to me. I also knew I wanted to get into accounting, so I was looking for schools with great accounting programs. I ended up visiting North Carolina, Wake Forest, Duke, and North Carolina State. When it came right down to it, I really got a great feel from North Carolina. It had the best accounting program of the four, and since I live in the state, tuition was very reasonable."

Not a bad response. Then on the other end of the spectrum, some students would say something like:

"Hmmm, I don't really know. My older sister went to UNC and when I went to visit her, I had a blast. The hoops team rocks, and it's a totally fun campus. Plus my mom thought it would be a good place for me."

Quite a bit different, wouldn't you say? In a behavioral interview, the recruiting director will continue to ask you about everything on your resume. The questions will be somewhat general, as she is trying to unearth what makes you tick. So, for instance, if you were president of your class, the recruiting director may ask you questions like:

- Why did you decide to run?
- Why do you think you were successful?
- What were you most proud of?

- What would you do differently if you could do it all over again?
- What would your VP say about you as a leader?
- What was the most difficult situation you faced and how did you handle it?

She can see from your resume that you were president. Now she wants to know all the juicy details. She may end up spending ten minutes just talking about your experience as president of your class.

Shocking Interview Confession #11
You need to know the ins and outs of every single thing on your resume.

Think through each entry on your resume, whether it's a major internship or just a club that you joined for a semester. Everything is fair game for the recruiting director to talk about. In fact, you may spend a majority of the interview talking about something you consider to be minor on your resume. You just never know. In general, here's what you want to think about for everything on your resume:

- Why did you get involved?
- What did you learn?
- What did you contribute?
- How did your experience differ from others around you?
- What would your boss/manager say about you?
- What would your coworkers/other students say about you?
- How would you do it differently if you had to do it all over again?

This may sound like torture to think about for everything on your resume, but having at least reacquainted yourself with these experiences will make the interview go so much more smoothly. Again, you don't want to memorize answers, but you do want to have this stuff top-of-mind. I can't tell you how many times I'd ask someone a basic question like "Why did you join the French Club?" and the answer would be "I don't really know. I just figured 'why not.'" That's no way to impress a recruiter!

Knowing what's on your resume is critically important, but, alas, you're bound to get a host of questions in an interview that have nothing to do with your resume. In fact, these killer questions may have nothing to do with anything you've *ever* done.

Shocking Interview Confession #12
Interviewers often ask tough questions just to see you sweat.

Not because they're cruel. We've hopefully already dispelled that notion. But the fact is, in the real world there will be countless occasions when you have to think on your feet, when you'll be challenged by a coworker, manager, or customer, when you will have to defend your opinion, or when you'll have to sell a point of view to a skeptical colleague or client.

Asking some of the questions below is a great way to test your grace under pressure and gauge how you might perform in the real world.

There are certain interview questions that everyone dreads. We already talked about the evil "What are your weaknesses?" question and how to answer it. I'm sure you've thought about a few other beasts and broke out into a cold sweat. Questions like:

- Tell me about yourself.
- Where do you see yourself in ten years?
- If you were stranded on a deserted island with only one book, what would it be and why?
- How many blades of grass are there on a football field?
- What color is your brain?
- Tell me one thing about you that you don't want me to know?
- Why did you play sports in college? I think it's a complete waste of time.

I can almost hear the screams of pain! But don't worry, we'll discuss why these questions are asked, what the recruiting director is looking for, and the best ways to answer all of them.

Let's look at these gems and talk about both the wrong way and the right way to respond.

1. TELL ME ABOUT YOURSELF.

Wrong

"I was born in 1986 in a small town in rural Minnesota. After a hard life of chopping wood and caring for the kinfolk, I moved to the big city when I was eleven. I broke my ankle chasing Tony Weisman through the trees that very year and was in a cast for six weeks. Boy, was that a pain in the neck. The next summer, I mostly spent at the pool and was practically addicted to kick the can in the neighborhood. Chris Gould was one of my best friends at the time and he and I were inseparable. We played a lot of Strat-O-Matic baseball inside, and football and soccer outside. That was a great summer, blah, blah, blah . . ."

By asking this question, a recruiting director is trying to get a sense of who you are and what you find to be important in your life. It's obviously an extremely open-ended question, and the interviewer is also attempting to see how you can take the ball and run with it.

Instead of regaling the interviewer with your entire life story, think about that question this way: Why am I sitting in this chair interviewing with this company right now?

Right

"I've been interested in finance and banking since I was fourteen years old. My dad actually gave me the business section to read and I fell in love with the stock market. I loved the numbers, the companies, and watching the market go up and down. When I was fifteen, I took five hundred dollars of savings from cutting lawns and invested it in my own portfolio. I'm pretty sure it was at that moment that I knew I was going to work in finance someday.

When it came time to pick a college, I knew I'd be studying finance, so that was an important factor in my school selection criteria. I decided that among the schools I was looking at, the University of Minnesota had the best finance program and allowed me to stay in state and save some money.

I've loved every second of it here, both inside and outside the classroom. Of course I am a finance major focusing on international markets, and I've really enjoyed the classes and my professors. I've had some great opportunities to use my finance background as treasurer of student government. By overhauling some of our procedures and processes, we were able to turn a six hundred dollar deficit into a four thousand dollar surplus during my term. I also was fortunate enough to have had a great internship at UBS in their corporate finance department this past summer. It was an incredible experience to be on Wall Street and see how the markets work firsthand. Now I'm anxious to parlay my experiences into a full time job with CitiBank. Oh, and that portfolio I started in 1991 with five hundred dollars is now worth more than four thousand dollars."

You should think about talking for about one minute or so. Again, not a dissertation on your entire life, but some good solid background that speaks to your skills and aptitude for the job.

2. WHERE DO YOU SEE YOURSELF IN TEN YEARS?

Wrong
"Wow, that's a tough one. I haven't really thought about it much. I suppose working here, and maybe a VP or something."

Wrong
"I figure I'll work here for a year or two and then go back to graduate school, get my MBA, and then start making some real money."

Right
"Advertising has always fascinated me, so I anticipate working in the field for a while. I've studied it quite a bit in school, and now I'm very anxious to dive in and learn more about how it works in the "real world." At a company like BBDO there are so many great accounts and so many great people that I'm sure I'd have the opportunity to learn and grow and contribute for a long time. In ten years time, I'd hope to be enjoying my career and serving as a valuable asset to the team in a management capacity."

Oftentimes students think that by asking this question recruiters want to hear that you are solely dedicated to their company for the rest of your career. And while they certainly don't want a response like wrong answer number two above, you don't need to declare a never-ending commitment to the organization. It's simply not realistic. The correct response above tells the recruiter you've at least thought about a career path, and you could indeed still be working at the company. Importantly, though, you want to impress upon them your desire to learn, grow, and contribute. What recruiting directors are interested in hearing is what kind of plan you have for your career and what your aspirations are, and if those aspirations are in line with what the company is all about. Plus, you'd be amazed at the number of people who come out with the wrong answers listed above. It makes it easy for recruiting directors to weed out a few people!

3. IF YOU WERE STRANDED ON A DESERTED ISLAND WITH ONLY ONE BOOK, WHAT WOULD IT BE AND WHY?

This one is no fun. It's a classic think-on-your-feet test. As we said above, companies want to see you how you react under situations that you may face in the workplace. No, of course no one will ask you this question on the job, but you will be faced with situations where you're standing in front of a group of people and have to answer an odd question or two.

And like most of these questions, there's not a right or wrong answer per se. In other words, they are not going to say, "Oh, you said the Bible and we were actually looking for Dante's *Inferno*. I'm sorry, you're not going to get the job." The question is less about what you actually answer, but more about how you think about it and justify your decision.

However, there is certainly a right and wrong way to approach this question. For some of these odd ones, you can start out with a joke to break the ice and to give yourself some more time to think. "Hmm, if I had only one book, it would have to be *Getting Yourself Rescued from a Deserted Island for Dummies.*" Then answer something, really anything, you want. What they are looking for is how you think through your response and the reasons for your decision.

Wrong

"Let's see, I'm not really sure. Maybe War and Peace *because it's long?"*

Right

"It's funny that you ask that because I actually was stranded on a deserted island for a while back in high school, and all I had was Who Moved My Cheese? *which was a big mistake. Way too short. Okay, I'm just kidding. If stranded, I would want a book that could serve a lot of purposes. It would have to be entertaining, stimulating, thought provoking, and in many ways serve as a companion to me. I'd probably go with Homer's* Illiad *in poetry form. It's an amazing tale, one of the great all-time classics, and certainly a very powerful book. I'm sure it would serve as a decent friend until we were both hopefully rescued."*

4. HOW MANY BLADES OF GRASS ARE THERE ON A FOOTBALL FIELD?

These types of questions tend to be more prevalent in consulting or banking interviews. Some other classics include:

- How many grains of sand are there on all the beaches of the world?
- How high would Lake Tahoe rise if you filled it with all the dog food in the United States?
- How long would it take you to walk from the top of Canada to the bottom of Argentina?

As with the "desert island" question above, the person interviewing you is less concerned about what you actually come up with and much more concerned about how you think through the problem. Take a second to collect your thoughts, have them repeat the question, and then talk the recruiting director through your thought process. Again, a quick little joke may help break the tension. With these questions, organizations are testing your ability to think critically, think strategically, and think quantitatively on your feet. It's acceptable to ask them if you can use pen and paper to figure out your answer, although they may deny your request!

Wrong

"Wow! I have absolutely no idea. I'm sure a lot, though. Probably millions."

Right

"I spent a couple of years cutting lawns back in high school. Now I'm wishing I had done a better job at counting the clippings. Okay, how many blades of grass on a football field? Well, a football field is 120 yards long with the end zones by about 50 yards across, or at least I think it's close to that. That means it's 6,000 square yards, or 54,000 square feet. Let's say a typical blade of grass is one-tenth of an inch. That means there are 120 or so in a foot, or 120 times 120 which is 14,400 in one square foot. Now 54,000 square feet times 14,400 is the total number of blades of grass. If I can use a pen and paper, I can give you an exact amount. Otherwise we can add five zeroes to 14,400 and cut it in half and then add a few to get about 750,000,000 blades, give or take a few million."

5. WHAT COLOR IS YOUR BRAIN?

Say what? This question falls into the incredibly bizarre camp. Here the recruiter is simply testing your creativity and your ability to deal with a question you could have never prepared for. Oftentimes interviewers will ask a question like this if they feel a candidate has been throwing out a lot of canned answers to typical questions. Here you just want to come up with something, anything that sounds decent and exhibits some creativity and original thought.

Wrong

"Gray. In high school we dissected a fetal pig and it was gray, so I figure a human brain is the same color."

Right

"What color is my brain? I can honestly say no one has asked me that one before. I'll need a second or two to figure this one out . . .

I guess my brain would be multicolored. A big part of it would be red, for passion. I'm passionate about a lot of things like success, work, relationships, and sports. Another part would be green. I like the outdoors, I consider myself something of an environmentalist, and I do enjoy green lights on the road as I have a tendency to drive a bit fast on occasion. All those things conjure green to me. Finally there would be some purple in there. I just like the color purple and I think it speaks to my creativity and my uniqueness. I'm not sure it would be a good-looking brain with all those colors, but it works for me!"

6. TELL ME ONE THING ABOUT YOU THAT YOU WOULDN'T WANT ME TO KNOW.

This is a somewhat veiled attempt to get at your weaknesses. Sometimes a recruiting director may ask this question if he didn't like your weakness answer. In any event, you want to think about it much the same way you think about the "What are your weaknesses?" question. One of the differences here is that you can use this to show how you turned a negative situation into a learning experience.

Wrong
"I once dropped a hamburger on the floor and then gave it to my roommate to eat without telling him."

Wrong
"I'm really bad at math. I mean seriously bad where I can't do simple addition without using a calculator. It's pretty scary."

Right
"I suppose I wouldn't want you to know that I probably didn't do the best job as a manager of people the first few times I held leadership positions. I tended to think that being a leader was pretty easy: I'd tell someone what to do, and they would do it. Hey, it seemed to work with my dad when he told me to do something! But pretty quickly I realized it doesn't work that way with my classmates. I discovered that being a good manager requires really understanding your team and what makes them tick. I found that I have to communicate better and

compromise more. I think I'm getting better at it, but it was pretty rough at the beginning!"

7. WHY DID YOU PLAY SPORTS IN COLLEGE? I THINK IT'S A COMPLETE WASTE OF TIME.

Just like you may get asked an odd question to see how you think on your feet, you may get asked a question like this to see how you defend your point of view. The fact is, no matter what job you go into, you'll have to defend your point of view. Maybe it's to sell a product to a client, maybe it's to convince your boss to try a new idea, or maybe it's to persuade your manager to give you a raise.

The interviewer may challenge you on anything that is obviously important to you based on your resume or what you've discussed in the interview. Similar questions include:

- Why did you go to the school you went to? Big universities are just graduation factories.
- Why were you so involved in student government? I'm sure you weren't able to make a significant impact on campus.
- Why did you join a sorority? They are all just elitist organizations.

The interviewer is not trying to pick a fight or make you mad. Instead, she is trying to gauge how you can defend your point of view and stand up for yourself in a difficult or pressure-packed situation. The key is to not back down, but to make your case in a compelling and respectful way.

Wrong
"Wow, you know you're right. What was I thinking spending four years playing tennis? What a total waste of time. I wish I had spoken with you four years ago."

Wrong
"Waste of time? What the hell would you know? Based on how you look, I doubt you could even hold a tennis racquet, let alone play the sport competitively!"

Right

"I understand how you might have that point of view, but for me, my experiences on the tennis team were invaluable. I learned a tremendous amount about teamwork and dedication. My commitment to the sport was huge. Between practice and matches, I spent more than forty hours a week on tennis. It was like holding a full-time job while going to school. I'm proud of the fact that with this commitment, I was still able to graduate in four years with strong academics and with involvement in activities like the finance club and student government.

Additionally, I learned quite a bit about what it's like to be a part of a team and how even in an individual sport like tennis, teamwork is the key to success. When I first started as a freshman, we had a divided team. There was a clique of some of the upperclassmen that did things their own way. We had a new coach that year who was able to break down the barriers and show us the importance of working together for a goal. I must say it was inspiring to see that year's team finish with the best record in more than ten years.

All told, being on the team was one of the most positive experiences I had in college, and certainly one that will help me make the transition into the working world."

I wish I could tell you that this covers every bizarre, think-on-your-feet question, but, alas, it wouldn't be true. By definition of the category, though, recruiting directors are going to be hurling a few gems like these out of left field. I'm sure you've learned, though, that what's important is not as much *what* you say but *how* you compose yourself and think about an answer. They are testing how cool you are in the face of adversity and your grace under pressure—real-world situations you are bound to face. They are not looking for the "right" answer, but they are looking for the right way to answer. Take your time, collect yourself, and come up with something, anything, and make it sound good.

Another tough question merits an entire discussion, and that's the salary question. Classics include:

- How much are you expecting to make?
- What are your salary expectations?
- What kind of salary do you think you deserve?

Chances are you'd probably prefer to have your fingernails plucked off one by one than answer questions like these. And trust me, your fear shows up in an interview.

Shocking Interview Confession #13
Students almost always answer the salary question wrong.

It's true. Even though you're definitely worried about how to answer some of the killer questions we just went over, I'm sure the salary question is the most daunting.

So why do recruiting directors even put you through this torture in the first place? There are two key reasons. First, they simply want to know how little they can get away with paying you. I know it sounds a bit devious, but it's true. Think about it this way: If you walked into a store and bought a stereo for five hundred dollars and you found out later they would have sold it to you for four hundred dollars, don't you wish you would have known that in advance?

Second, they want to see if your expectations are in line with what the job offers. In other words, if you expect to be making thirty-five thousand dollars and the job only pays twenty-five thousand dollars, they probably aren't going to want to hire you. They figure you'll feel as if you are underpaid from the get-go and you'll constantly complain about your salary. Or you'll look to leave the company for a better-paying job at the first possible chance.

Welcome to the real world. No one is looking out for you and making sure life is fair. You're on your own now, and many of the stories of dog eat dog are true. Now that's not to say it's pure evil out there. Most companies have set salaries for entry-level hires, so you won't have to worry about answering the salary question, but you do need to be prepared in case you do get it.

Preparation is the key to dealing with the salary question. The first thing you want to do is a bit of homework (sorry!). Before you go on interviews, get a sense for what salaries are in your field. You can check out Monster, Yahoo!, and other career sites where they list salary statistics. Also, the US Department of Labor Statistics has average salaries for jobs.

Finally, trade publications for the industries you're entering typically have annual salary survey results.

Like any good negotiator (and that's what asking about salary is, a negotiation instigated by the company), you don't want to start by throwing out any numbers. In the "Sealing the Deal" chapter we discuss some negotiation strategies upon receiving an offer, and you can tap into some of the same techniques here. So if you get the question "What do you think you should be earning?" here are a couple of ways to respond:

Wrong
"I don't know. I'm desperate for a job, so whatever you guys think is cool with me."

Wrong
"I would say six figures. I'm worth at least that."

Right
"Salary is definitely important to me, but ultimately I would judge any offer based on all of the benefits, including salary. It would be tough for me to throw out a figure without being able to see the entire package."

Right
"I would hope to make in the range of what someone with my background and experiences would deserve based on the job responsibilities."

Sometimes the old I'm-not-going-to-throw-out-a-number trick will work just fine. But to be honest, sometimes it won't. The recruiting director may insist that you give him a salary figure. In those instances, knowing your facts is the key. So, if you give the recruiter one of the "Right" answers listed above, and then he fires back, "I actually want to know specifically what salary you're looking for," here's what you say:

Wrong
"Hmm, how about $30,000?"

Right

"Based on research that I have done, the average salary for an entry-level production assistant in New York City is twenty-five thousand to thirty-five thousand dollars, and I would expect my salary to be in that range."

Being forced to answer the salary question clearly puts you in a tough spot. You need a plan of attack on how to deal with it for every interview. The key is knowing what the salary ranges are and ultimately deciding what you're willing to earn.

It's one thing to have to answer all of these tough questions in your traditional one-on-one situation. The stakes can be higher and the surroundings even more difficult in some nontraditional interview settings.

Shocking Interview Confession #14
Nontraditional interviewing situations are becoming increasingly more common.

The classic interview features two people sitting across from each other for thirty minutes, separated by a nice mahogany desk. In many instances, this may be your exact interviewing scenario. However, as companies look to work more efficiently, there has been a movement to a whole range of interviewing situations.

THE PHONE INTERVIEW

On the plus side, now you can finally interview in your underwear! On the negative side, it's much more difficult to sell yourself.

Shocking Interview Confession #15
You have to work much harder in a phone interview to show your personality and excitement.

In an in-person interview, the recruiting director can see your face, your body language, and your expressions. He'll catch a smile on your face, a twinkle in your eye, or even a sense of excitement or intrigue. On the phone, he tends to get a monotone boring candidate.

It's true. You lose a lot of your personality over the phone, and the issues we talked about before, regarding being too formal and stiff in an interview, can get even worse. Fight hard to let your real self shine through.

When you have a phone interview, make sure you are animated and smile a lot. It sounds silly, but it can make a huge difference to the person on the other end of the phone. Use hand gestures, and try to move around a bit, even standing up on occasion to reinforce a point. If you can get one of those hands-free headsets (like the friendly Time-Life operators wear on TV) definitely do it. This allows you to have even more body language freedom.

Another good tip is to put your interviewing suit on for a phone interview. I know it sounds crazy, but it helps get you in the game. Remember, a little bit of nervous energy is a good thing.

Never conduct a phone interview on a cell phone. It's simply too risky in terms of call quality, background noise, and battery life. Similarly, if you're using a cordless phone, make sure it's charged up to the max. "Sorry, my phone is about to die" is not a great way to end an interview.

Finally, be prepared for a potentially very long phone call. Most phone interviews are about thirty to forty-five minutes long, but in some instances they can stretch on to more than an hour. For some people that's an incredibly long period to be talking on the phone. At the risk of being stereotypical, some guys may have *never* been on the phone that long in their lives. You may discover that after about thirty minutes your ear goes numb, or it hurts so bad you want to cry. It's much better to discover that little fact *before* you have an interview. Practice makes perfect. Call your mom, call your dad, call a friend, call anyone, and talk to them for up to an hour to see what it's like. Have some water with you as well, since you'll be doing a lot of the talking. Just don't drink too much, especially since you'll be constrained by a land line!

THE GANG-UP

At some companies, they don't believe that one interviewer is enough. They will have three or four people interview you at the same time. Seems a bit more like a trial and less like an interview!

Recruiting directors do this for a few reasons. One, it *is* a bit like a trial, and much like we've discussed before, part of the interview is intended to see how you perform under pressure and in unfamiliar situations. I have a feeling that for most of you, being interviewed by three people at once would fall into the camp of pressured and unfamiliar. The second reason for multiple interviews is simply one of efficiency. Companies can get more of their employees exposed to more candidates in a shorter period of time. Finally, having all the interviewers in the room at the same time makes comparing notes after the interview much easier. Companies avoid situations like "Well, gosh, he had a great interview with me. I wonder why he didn't with you."

So what do you do when faced with a panel of interviewers? At the risk of sounding like a broken record, be yourself, be composed, and try to have some fun. But here are a few specific tips to help you out:

Pay Attention to Eye Contact

Even though one person is asking a question, you need to include all the interviewers in the room with your answer. As you respond to a question, look directly into the eyes of the person who asked the question, but once you get going, look decisively at the other folks. Try to end the question looking back at the original interviewer. That being said, make meaningful eye contact. Don't simply bob your head from person to person with each word that you say.

Stay Focused

While good interviews tend to be conversational, gang-up interviews tend to be a bit more disjointed. It's hard for a discussion to flow as much when questions are being lobbed from all over. As a result, you need to concentrate harder on what is being asked and how you respond. Don't be surprised if the same question is asked multiple times, but just worded slightly differently by the other interviewers. You don't want to say, "Actually, Bob just asked that question." Instead, just repeat what you've already said, but use different language.

Intensify Your Energy and Enthusiasm

Because the interview is more like a battery of questions, and less like a discussion, you want to exude as much passion and interest as possible. It's more difficult to create a rapport with a group of people than it is with just one individual. Your natural tendency is to act a bit like a boxer who's getting creamed by an opponent. You take your blow and then just wait for the next one. Instead, be excited, be interested, and make sure you do small things like smile a lot, stay aggressive, and sit up attentively in your chair. The blows won't seem so painful!

Remember the Interviewers

You may think of the interviewers amorphously as the "Legion of Doom" or another disparaging collective moniker. But actually these are real, distinct people. After the interview, you'll have to write them each a thank-you note, and each letter will have to be different. The chapter on thank-you notes will tell you how to write a great note, but you'll want to say something unique to each person. Remember who said what, remember the questions they asked, and remember how they responded to you. The best way to do this is to take notes *immediately* after the interview on their business cards.

THE MARATHON

The endless day of interviewing is still an approach that most companies take. Often called a "full round" or "office visit," it entails your undertaking several one-on-one interviews in succession, usually after you've already interviewed with the company on campus or over the phone. These interviews will typically be held at the company's office and comprise interviews with people at all levels within the organization. This can range anywhere from two to eight interviews in a day.

It's a tough day for sure. If you thought one interview was bad, now you get the chance to tack on a bunch more, in succession! But much like a marathon, preparation is the key. First of all, be prepared to talk . . . a lot! You can and will be asked about anything. All the advice dispensed above about preparation is key. Also, you may be asked the same questions by different interviewers. It's important to stay excited and focused during the entire day. I'm sure you'll be saying to yourself by the fourth interview, "If I have to talk about my internship at General Electric one more time, I'm going to shoot myself!" But remember, even though you're telling the story for the fourth time, the interviewer is just hearing it for the first time. You have to respond with the same passion and emotion as you did initially.

Because you are doing a lot of talking, make sure you drink some water. Below we talk about fluids and how to deal with them, but just make sure you get something to drink because you will get dry mouth. And nobody likes to interview with dry mouth!

Get a good night's sleep. I know it goes without saying, but you will be exhausted by the end of the day. You may be visiting a new city and want to check it out, or you may even have the chance to go out with some representatives from the company, but remember, it's all about the interview and not about having the time of your life. No one will think it's cool if you interview hung over.

Speaking of company representatives, sometimes an organization will invite you in for an extended trip to interview, visit the company, and learn about the city you may be moving to. They'll put you up in a nice hotel, match you up with some more junior people for lunch and dinner, and may even allow you to go exploring on your own. These all add up to the potential for danger! Remember, everything you do on this trip—whether it's interviewing with a VP or going out for dinner with someone a year older than you—is likely to be scrutinized by the company. At my former job we saw it all. We had candidates who:

- Emptied out a hotel minibar and charged it to the company
- Ran up hundreds of dollars in long-distance phone calls
- Got drunk and threw up on their pre-interview dinner
- Hit on existing employees

Needless to say, none of them received offers!

Finally, we mentioned just above about remembering your interviewers, and the same advice holds true here. Make sure to ask for a business card after each interview and quickly jot down some notes as soon as you have a second. Even if it's something as simple as what the interviewer is wearing, you'll need notes to remember what you talked about.

THE MEAL

It's bad enough that they're interviewing you, and it's bad enough that you have to dress up in a suit, but now they add the "pleasure" of doing it over a meal, so they can put you in an even more uncomfortable position! Again, it's all about grace under pressure and it's all about your presence. Don't freak out and you'll do just fine. Here are some tips:

It's Not About the Food

You might be thinking. "If they want to interview me over lunch, at least I'll get a free meal out of it and I LOVE lobster tails." Alas, that's not a good approach to take. You actually want to remove food from the equation and have it more about what you have to say. You do not want to call attention to what you're ordering or how you are eating it.

Be very conservative in what you order. Obviously stay away from ribs, spaghetti, or other "problem" foods. The last thing you need is marinara sauce down the front of your shirt. As for what to actually order, try to defer to the other person. If the waiter comes by to take your order, just say, "I haven't decided yet. Can you start with her?" That way you'll know what you should expect to order both in terms of food choices and number of courses. If the interviewer gets a salad and a main course, then you can as well. Watch for the price ranges too. You don't want to be ordering the filet mignon if she just got a club sandwich. Of course you don't need to order exactly what the interviewer does, but you should stay in the same price range.

Watch your manners as well. Remember what mom taught you. Put your napkin in your lap, chew with your mouth closed, keep your elbows off the table, and don't talk while eating. The last one may be tricky simply because if it's an interview, you might be asked a lot of questions. Remember, it's NOT about the food, so if you have to sit there with your glorious baked salmon barely touched, so be it.

Oftentimes a more junior member of the team may be taking you out on the lunch or dinner. It may be a more casual environment and seem less like an interview. Even so, rest assured that you are still being evaluated. Watch the funny stuff. Questions like "Is it okay if I have a beer?" or "Do you mind if I smoke?" don't go over very well. Also avoid being too casual and saying things like "Oh, I only plan to work here for about a year, and then go back and get my MBA." Remember, it's still an interview.

In an interview, everything you say and do has an impact on your performance. Don't think that the interviewer isn't noticing everything.

Shocking Interview Confession #16
**Things like what you wear, your handshake, and
when you show up can ultimately make a big
difference when it comes down to deciding
between an offer and a rejection.**

Typically these minor points only affect you when you do something *wrong,* but trust me, many students mess up on these "small" things. Below is the straight scoop on the preinterview, the interviewer's perspective, and an approach for the day.

ATTIRE

This one almost always is way tougher than it needs to be. Dress is something that should not be a determining factor in your candidacy. The best way to think about it is that you really don't want anyone to notice your attire one way or another.

You should wear a suit (and tie for men) to every interview. Period. The only rare exception is when the company specifically tells you not to wear a suit. If the company is casual, you still wear a suit. I like to call it corporate hazing—"Hey, look at the new guy interviewing in his suit!" But seriously, dressing appropriately shows respect for the company. If you underdress for an interview, the downside is huge. If you overdress for an interview, the downside is minimal.

So now, what type of suit do you wear? This can be a bit trickier. The more conservative the field, the more conservative your attire. For industries like law, banking, and consulting, men will want to go with a classic dark suit, plain white or blue shirt, and subdued tie. Women will typically want to go with a dress suit with conservative hem length. If you are applying for a job in more liberal fields like PR, advertising, entertainment, and production, you have a bit more flexibility in what you can wear. Women can go with a pantsuit or a skirt suit. Men should still wear a suit and tie, but they do have some leeway to go with more interesting colors—not too crazy, though. But don't feel like you *have* to go nuts. Being more conservative is always the safer route.

I suggest you buy a well-made, year-round, 100 percent wool suit and then buy a few different blouses/shirts (and ties) to mix it up a bit. There may be times when you interview multiple times with a company. You're not expected to have a different suit each time, but a new shirt and/or tie can give you a totally different look.

Make sure your clothes are nicely pressed. The few bucks a dry cleaner charges to iron your shirt is money well spent! Be sure your shoes are polished and clean. Finally, men need to be certain that their socks are long enough so that when they sit down and cross their legs, they don't flash disgusting hairy calf flesh to the interviewer!

Perhaps most importantly with attire, *do not* wear any of your interview clothes for the first time on the interview! It sounds weird, but test your clothes out. You may find that the new shoes make your feet bleed after about twenty minutes, that your suit itches so badly you feel like you have poison ivy, that your tie chokes off all circulation to your head, or that your blouse puckers when you sit down. It's much better to figure that out *before* the interview starts!

ACCESSORIES

Plan on bringing something to write with and to hold about five extra copies of your resume. You don't need a briefcase, but don't walk in with your ratty backpack, canvas messenger bag, or frilly purse. I suggest a "padfolio" which can hold the essential items you need. Women can also bring a purse if they would like, but again, make sure it's professional.

Another accessory area of concern is what I call "body accessories." Yes, the ever popular tongue studs, colored hair, and various body piercings. Students will often ask me, "Do I have to remove my eyebrow ring before I interview." And I say, "Only if you want a job." Again, much of it depends on the field you are going into. For instance, if you are applying for a job at a body piercing company, or as a groupie for a punk rock band, then by all means pierce away! But for virtually every other job out there—even ones in creative fields—you run the risk of rubbing people the wrong way with the weird stuff.

Students will sometimes say, "I'm an individual, and I want to stand out. I don't want to be a corporate drone like everyone else. I'm sure once they see my Mohawk, they'll recognize that I'm a revolutionary with the big ideas that will take the company to the next level." Wouldn't it be great if that were true? Remember, you haven't proven yourself at a company yet and are trying to make a good impression in the first interview. If you are Bill Gates and you want to wear a pink tutu to work, that's fine, but until you've established yourself, you'd be much better off standing out as the guy who gave the great interview and not the guy who wore the spiked dog collar.

For every ten people you may interview with, one may think your revolutionary ways are cool, one may not care one way or another, but in all probability, the other eight are going to think it's completely inappropriate. That being said, it's ultimately a personal choice. I once worked with a woman who was applying for a job in marketing, and she said she wore a nice suit with a bright red shirt to her interview. It was certainly professional, but not ultraconservative. She felt like that may have been part of the reason she didn't get the job. But ultimately she decided she didn't want to work for a company that would look down upon someone wearing a red shirt! The attire/accessory decision is completely yours, but remember, the more risks you take, the more you limit your job options.

ARRIVAL TIME

You have the sweet suit on, and it's time to head out for the job interview. When do you leave and when should you arrive? One of the most obvious pieces of advice you will ever hear is "Do not be late for an interview." No duh, right? Yet you would be amazed at the number of college students who do indeed show up late for an interview. Obviously, a majority of those candidates are currently unemployed.

If you know you can make it from campus to downtown San Francisco in thirty-five minutes with no traffic and by hitting all the lights, DO NOT leave for the interview thirty-five minutes ahead of time. It's simply unacceptable to walk in late to an interview and say, "Sorry, dude, traffic was a bitch today." The interview is you at your best. If you can't show up on time for an interview, then what are you going to be like on the job? You should leave at least twice as much time as it would conservatively take you to get to the job interview.

That being said, do not then arrive at the receptionist desk two hours before your interview. You should plan to arrive about five to ten minutes in advance of the interview. If you do arrive at the location two hours early, drive around the block, read the paper, but wait before you go in. Remember, though, at some larger office buildings in cities like New York, Chicago, and Los Angeles, it may take you awhile to get through security and be escorted to the office, so leave extra time.

THE HANDSHAKE

The moment has become real. They have called your name and you are now first meeting the person who will be doing the grilling for the next thirty minutes. She holds out her hand for the handshake. Sadly, this is the beginning of the end for some candidates.

There's an old dandruff ad where they say, "You never get a second chance to make a first impression." And like most ads, they speak the truth! Studies have shown that the first sixty seconds often make the most important impression in an interview, or really in just about any social situation. Think about it. When you meet people at a party, you make decisions about them from the moment you lay eyes on them and start to talk. Some of the impressions are conscious, and some are unconscious: that guy seemed arrogant, that girl sounded smart, or that guy was so nice. It's the same in an interview.

When you approach the interviewer, look him in the eye, walk with confidence, and then shake his hand like a pro. For those of you who are experienced handshakers, you know how off-putting it is to get a weak handshake. The worst ones are the "dead fish" shakes where someone just lays his hand in yours but doesn't squeeze. Another classic is the half handshake where people fold their hands in half and just give you the top part of their hands to shake. I assume they want me to bow down and kiss their hands as if we were in Victorian England!

Finally, if you suffer from perpetually sweaty or clammy hands, here's a trick. Get to the interview a few minutes early. Ask to go to the bathroom, and then proceed to wash your hands in hot, soapy water (and obviously dry them completely). The hot, soapy water will dry your hands out a bit, at least long enough to shake that first hand.

Here's how a good handshake works. The webbing between your thumb and forefinger should meet up with their webbing. Give it a nice squeeze (not too hard though . . . we don't want broken bones) and pump it about four times and release. It sounds easy, but 20 percent of the handshakes I got from college students left a bad first impression. This may sound weird, but practice your handshakes. Shake hands with some friends and family, and ask for feedback. Since they're your friends, they hopefully won't think you're a freak!

Don't go overboard with the handshake either. Don't use two hands. Don't put a second hand up on the forearm, and for heaven's sake, no hugging or cheek kissing! A confident, well-done handshake helps get the interview off on the right foot.

FLUIDS

The first question you are often asked in an interview is one of the most perplexing to college students. The interviewer says, "Hey, Letty, would you like something to drink?" A jolt of pain shoots through your body! You probably think:

"Hmm, I'm sure that's some type of deceitful question the recruiter uses to trick college students. If I say yes, then that means that I'll be perceived as being high maintenance and demanding. I'm sure they don't want that. But if I say no, they'll think I'm hard to please and don't go along with the group and with others. Oh, the inhumanity! How can this evil interviewer do this to me?"

Here's the earth-shattering advice for such a difficult question. If you're thirsty, say yes; if not, say no. Guess what? It's not a trick question. It's just the interviewer being polite. Hard to believe, but true. I actually do suggest that you take her up on her offer, since you will probably be doing a lot of talking in the interview, and it will be nice to have a drink. Also, if you do take a drink, make sure it's water. In the unlikely event of a major spill, it's pretty embarrassing to be walking around with a huge coffee stain on your nice white shirt, or to have dumped a sticky Coke on the interviewer's desk.

If you do drink a lot of water, then there's the other fluid issue you have to consider. Most interviewers will ask you if you need to use the restroom, especially if you have multiple interviews within the same company. In the event that they do not ask, and in the event that you run the risk of bursting some vital organ, it's perfectly acceptable at the beginning of the interview to ask, "Do you mind if I use the restroom before we start?" Trust me, it's not a big deal, and decidedly better than the alternative!

That sums up the little things. With a bit of preparation, and the right mind-set, you should have no problem going into the interview prepared and confident.

So you're ready to enter the interview relaxed and ready to go. The next big question is, What's the interviewer thinking?

Shocking Interview Confession #17
You and the interviewer have a decidedly different perspective on the interview.

For you, an interview is often one of the biggest days of your life. We're talking about your future here, and the ability to convince a company to pay you tens of thousands of dollars. For them it's just another thirty-minute meeting in the course of a day. For you, the preparation has been underway for days or even weeks. You've splurged on the new business suit, you've practiced interviewing, you've researched the company, you've mapped out a plan to arrive in plenty of time, you've bought your new padfolio, and you've removed your tongue stud. For them it's just another thirty-minute meeting. Sad, but true. During any typical day, an interviewer may have a few meetings, may have a big presentation due by the close of business, and may have just come out of a meeting where he was chewed out by his boss. In virtually every instance, the interview isn't even the most important meeting of the day for the interviewer, let alone the most important meeting of his life.

As a result, not enough individuals take the time to adequately prepare before conducting an interview. But knowing this fact and knowing what to expect can help you make a favorable impression given the circumstances. Here's what to look out for from interviewers:

PREPARATION

Sure, you've spent quite a bit of time on your resume, but don't assume that interviewers have necessarily even read it. They will most likely have a copy with them, but just to be sure, bring a few extra resumes for every interview. The first question you're asked could be something like "Where did you go to school?" or "Have you ever held a leadership position?" You don't want to say, "Hey, dude, the first thing listed under the experience section is my position as president of the student body at Wesleyan University!"

Your best bet is to assume the interviewer hasn't had a chance to look at your resume, so don't worry about mentioning something that should be obvious, and don't freak out and take it personally that the interviewer hasn't read your resume.

INTERRUPTIONS

Most often when you are interviewing, it's in the middle of the business day at company offices. The phones are ringing, there may be customers in the building, and a host of "normal business day" activities are occurring. To be sure, some interviewers will close their door and focus intently during the interview, but in many cases this does not happen. As a result, your interviewer may be quite distracted. Physically, she may have to take a phone call, or someone may interrupt the interview to ask for her time. Mentally, she may be preoccupied because she has a huge assignment due right after your interview or may have screwed up at a meeting earlier in the day. Sadly, the business world doesn't just stop when it's time for your interview.

"Good afternoon, everyone, this is the CEO speaking. Tyler Mitchell is interviewing here today at 2:00. Now he's a college student, so we need to be on our best behavior. Samantha, I want all calls diverted directly into voice mail, and, Adele, make sure no one enters or leaves the building. Everyone needs to respect his time when he's here. Remember, he's a college student!"

Since this is clearly not the case, here are a couple of tips. One, stay focused during the interview. If for some reason your interviewer does get interrupted with a phone call, simply remember where you left off the conversation, and then bring the interviewer back up to speed. "We were talking about my experience in the finance club at college and how that helped prepare me for a career here."

Second, don't take it personally when something doesn't go according to plan. If the interview starts late, if the company substitutes interviewers at the last minute, or even if an interruption takes half of your interview time, simply go with the flow and do your best. It's another way to show your poise and your grace under pressure.

At some point you'll sense that the interview is mercifully finally coming to a close. It's no time to take a breather though.

Shocking Interview Confession #18
The end of the interview can make or break your candidacy.

Here are a couple of tips for you as you finish your time with the lovely person who has been grilling you:

QUESTIONS

Asking good questions at the end of the interview plays a big role in the hiring decision. Virtually every interviewer will close your session by saying, "Do you have any questions for me?" The absolute worst thing you can say is "no." It sends a message that you are not inquisitive and you don't have the insight to find out more about the company. Remember, the company is making a huge commitment to you, and you're making a huge commitment to it if you take the job. You should always have questions to ask.

That being said, you shouldn't have seventeen questions, but you should have about two or three. Even if you're interviewing with several people in the same day, you should always have a few questions for each interviewer. Please make sure these are not basic questions that you can learn about on their Web site or elsewhere. Also, you should never ask about salary during an interview. We have an entire section of the book on how to deal with salary questions, but the first rule is avoid asking about it at all costs. Ultimately the questions you ask should be about things you are legitimately interested in learning and discovering. The questions can fall into two camps: personal/job related and business related.

Personal/Job Related

Try to find out about the position, the company, and the culture of the company with questions like:

- What do you like about working here?
- What do you enjoy most about the job?
- What do you find frustrating about the job?
- What makes a new employee successful here?
- What are the best parts of the company culture?
- If you could change one thing about the company, what would it be?
- What is the career path like?
- What will my day-to-day activities entail?

These types of questions are great for finding out more about the job and exactly what you're getting into. If you discover that one of the skills that makes someone successful is the ability to present in front of large audiences, and you hate presenting, you may not want the job. The other nice thing about these questions is that you can ask them to different people in the company and get very different responses.

Business Related

These questions give you useful information about the business and the industry and also help you find out more about the company. Of course these will be very specific to the industry or the company you're applying to, but for a sense of what the questions can be like, here are a few:

- How has outsourcing affected your business?
- There's been a lot of consolidation in the industry. Do you think that's helped or hurt customer service?
- You've managed to grow while other companies have contracted. To what do you attribute that?
- How has the uncertain economy affected your business?

Again, tailor these to the types of jobs you are interviewing for.

Importantly, make sure you listen to the answers given. A common complaint I've heard from recruiting directors is that students just ask the questions because they were told to ask questions. They don't really care about the answers! A good trick is to ask another question based on the response they give. A great question-and-answer session at the end of an interview really gives you a chance to leave a powerful last impression.

NEXT STEPS

You should always leave an interview knowing when you're going to hear back from a company. If that information is not volunteered by your interviewer, it's perfectly acceptable to ask, "When can I expect to hear back from you regarding next steps?" It helps you know when to start bugging them if they have not contacted you.

Arguably, interviewing is the single most important part of the job-search process. Yes, you need a great resume and cover letter to get an interview, and yes, a thank-you note and your follow-up skills can help you seal the deal. But ultimately, the interview is where the rubber hits the road.

There's a lot of work to do to prepare for an interview, but now that you know what the companies, interviewers, and recruiting directors are thinking, you'll be in great shape to ace the interview.

Remember, ultimately an interview is just two human beings having a discussion! And once you ace that discussion, you'll need to write a thank-you note. Check out the next chapter for all the juicy details.

FIVE

Thank-You Notes— Finalizing the Sale

Four Shocking Confessions to Help You Leave a Lasting Impression

You've networked your way into a company, you've crafted a great cover letter and resume, and you've honed your interviewing skills and just spent hours being grilled by senior managers. Will the madness ever end?

Not just yet.

There's one more piece to the puzzle to help you land that job. Remember the prize: some company out there is going to pay you tens of thousands of dollars!

Shocking Thank-You-Note Confession #1
You must send a thank-you note after your interview.

The only reason this is a shocking fact is because most students don't do it. In fact, it's estimated that fewer than 25 percent of candidates who interview actually send a thank-you note. Shame on them!

The thank-you note can be an incredible tool to help you close the deal. It's your last chance to impress the company and convince them you're their candidate of choice. It's a huge opportunity that far too often goes completely missed.

When candidates interview with companies, the decision of whom to hire often isn't cut and dry. At my former company, by the time someone had finished interviewing, they had met with nine different people through first- and second-round interviews. Some companies out there will have you interview with more than a dozen people before all is said and done.

Rarely does a candidate ace all nine (or twelve or six or whatever the number) interviews. Additionally, companies are interviewing more candidates than they have open positions. You're in competition with others.

As a result, sometimes it's the little things that have a big impact when it comes to giving students an offer, whether they are competing against other candidates or not.

Shocking Thank-You-Note Confession #2
A thank-you note can make the difference between offer or rejection.

Think about it this way. You're the recruiting director and you're trying to decide whom to hire, Connor or Lindsey. They both did equally well in the interviews, they both have similar backgrounds, and they both would make great choices. But you only have one opening. Lindsey sends a great thank-you note, and Connor doesn't send one at all. Whom would you hire? Hopefully that settles the issue of whether or not you need to send a thank-you note.

Like everything else you've learned in this book, it's not enough just to send *any* thank-you note. It has to be a good, well-written one.

Shocking Thank-You-Note Confession #3
Thank-you notes must be short, personal, and interesting.

You want to make sure you reference something you talked about in the interview so it doesn't come off as generic. Most students send boring, rote thank-you notes that don't have a big impact.

Here's a typical example:

Dear Mr. Smith:

Thank you so much for the interview yesterday. I really enjoyed meeting you and learning more about the company. I hope you consider me for employment.

Regards,

Steve Brown

It's obvious why a thank-you note like this one doesn't work. That letter could have been written in your sleep.

So what exactly do you say? Like so much in life, we can go back to what Mom taught us as an example.

Remember when you were a ten-year-old sitting at the kitchen table trying to write thank-you notes for the birthday gifts you received? Talk about a painful memory! See if this scenario sounds familiar.

MOM: *Have you written your thank-you notes yet?*
KID: *No, but why do I have to write a thank-you note to Aunt Ruth?*
MOM: *Because she spent a lot of time and effort to buy you a gift.*
KID: *Fine! I just wrote it. Is that enough?*
MOM: *What do you have?*
KID: *"Dear Aunt Ruth, thank you for the new soccer ball."*
MOM: *No.*
KID: *But I don't know what else to say!*
MOM: *Well, have you used the soccer ball yet?*
KIDS: *Sure. I scored a goal with it against Shelby Adler.*
MOM: *There you go. Tell her all about it.*

Ah, the wisdom of a mother follows you your entire life. In essence that's exactly what you want to think about as you put together a thank-you note for a job.

Talk about something you discussed in the interview, talk about a salient point that was raised, or talk about something that stuck with you after the meeting. Just make sure it's personal and interesting. As with cover letters, keep two points in mind:

1. There's a fine line between clever and stupid.

2. Tailor your message to the person, to the company, and to the field.

You have more leeway to be creative based on the industry you've interviewed with. For jobs where you'll be judged on your creativity and your writing skills, by all means write an entertaining and (somewhat) edgy thank-you note. For more conservative fields, dial it back a bit. Remember, though, just because a field is conservative doesn't mean your thank-you note should be boring.

Here's an example of a well-written thank-you note:

Dear Mr. Schwartz,

It was an absolute pleasure to meet with you today. I have to say, it was amazing to finally see Accenture after all I had read and heard about it.

Our discussion about what makes companies successful really intrigued me. I've spent some more time thinking about it, and I truly feel that strong management, a thriving corporate culture, and great ideas are what set the best companies apart.

As for me, I couldn't be more excited about meeting with the team yesterday. From how welcomed I felt to the interesting people I met to the great discussions, I loved every second of it.

I'm very much looking forward to hearing back from you and hope that I can soon be a part of the team.

Thank you again for your time.

Regards,

Jasper Ryan

Just like the thank-you note to Aunt Ruth for the soccer ball, this letter shows the reader that you took the time to write something personal, that you remembered what you discussed and can comment on it, and ultimately that you were polite enough to do the correct thing and send a letter thanking someone for their time.

Now above I mentioned that at some companies you'll interview with several people all in the same day. In that case, do you have to send each and every one of them a thank-you note? And does each note have to be different? You don't want to hear the answer, do you? YES to both! You do need to send everyone a note, and they all need to be different.

In fact, one of the great challenges during a "full round" of interviews is even remembering what you talked about in each interview. Trust me, by the fourth or fifth interview in one day, you'll have trouble remembering your own name, much less which interviewer talked about your rock collection and which interviewer asked you about the future of the aeronautics industry.

Here's a trick. After each interview, make sure to ask the person for a business card, and jot down a few notes on the back of it. We talked about this in the interviewing chapter. Write down the main points you discussed in the interview or even what the interviewer was wearing—something that you can go back to in order to help you recall what was said. Importantly, you'll also have a name, address, and other information for sending out the thank-you note.

You may think you'll remember each person and what was discussed, but you won't. Trust me on this one.

Now that you have the information, when should you have the note to them?

Shocking Thank-You-Note Confession #4
You must have the thank-you note to the interviewer within twenty-four hours.

The truth is, companies typically make hiring decisions very rapidly. Or at least the interviewers make up their minds about candidates pretty quickly.

There is absolutely no benefit to delaying on this. As a result I recommend e-mailing your thank-you notes as soon as you possibly can. There's no reason you can't e-mail a thank-you note the night of the interview, if you can get back to your computer that quickly. At the very least, send it off the next day.

While I think handwritten notes can be a nice touch, it's the content that's more important than the look. A well-written thank-you note will definitely have an impact whether it's handwritten, typed, or e-mailed.

If you can get handwritten notes back to the company the next day by dropping them off, that's certainly an option, but don't feel that you must do this to make an impact. An e-mail is just fine.

The body of the e-mail can suffice as the thank-you note itself. There's no need to attach the thank-you note as an attachment in Word or any other format. In fact, you're better off staying away from attachments altogether. Given the current state of antispam and antivirus software, some corporate computer systems may reject your e-mail and not even notify you.

A NICE TOUCH

Oftentimes there may be a person whom you deal with in the interview process but who doesn't actually interview you. It may be a junior employee who takes you out to lunch, maybe a coordinator or assistant who makes all of your travel plans, or maybe even a receptionist whom you get to know better than your roommate because you spend a lot of time sitting in the waiting area!

It's a great idea to send that person a thank-you note as well. Again, as Mom once advised, you can't ever be too polite.

It makes sense for a couple of reasons. One, these people do spend quite a bit of time and effort to help you with the interview process, and two, you never know how connected they are to the hiring process. To be sure, in some instances the person making the hiring decision may not ever know that you sent a nice note to the receptionist. Then again, that receptionist may be a close friend of the recruiting director. In that case it certainly wouldn't hurt your candidacy to have the receptionist walk into the recruiting director's office, and say, "Boy, I really liked that woman Mollie. She sent me the nicest thank-you note!" As we mentioned above, these small things can make a huge difference when it comes time to make the final hiring decision.

Here's an example of one of those thank-you notes:

Dear Michele,

I just wanted to thank you so much for setting up all of my travel plans for the trip to Minneapolis last week. I know you spent a lot of time dealing with my flights. I guess I never realized how complicated it was to fly from Tuscaloosa, Alabama, to the Twin Cities!

Of course, it was also a special treat to be able to stay at the Grand Hotel. It's not often I sleep on a bed that nice. It's a far cry from my studio apartment. You certainly won't catch me complaining about the breakfast either.

I had an amazing time at the company and was really glad we finally had a chance to meet in person after all the phone calls and e-mails. I hope we have the opportunity to work together very soon.

Thanks again for all of your help. I truly do appreciate it.

Regards,

Mollie Melemed

The same rules apply to this type of letter as well—short, personal, and meaningful. You also want to send it out within twenty-four hours.

Don't think of thank-you notes as an afterthought. When it comes to making the hiring decision, for the recruiting director, thank-you notes can often play a big role.

Now that the hiring decision is in the hands of the company, what can you do to help it along? Read Chapter 6 to find out.

SIX

Sealing the Deal-Walking the Fine Line Between Persistent and Stalker

Ten Shocking Confessions to Help You Land the Job

Getting a job is a bit like one of those treasure hunts from the movies. You've traversed the world near and far, you've solved all the riddles and puzzles, and you've slayed the dragon and defeated the evil pirate. Lying before you is the treasure chest of untold riches. You reach down, open the latch, and what do you find? Yet another clue and another challenge!

So, just because you've created an amazing resume, researched companies, networked like crazy, written a great cover letter, dominated the interview, and crafted a fabulous thank-you note, you're still not done! This chapter covers the steps you need to take to make sure you get the job: following up with the company, evaluating your offer, and negotiating your salary.

You would think that at the end of the interview, the next steps would be pretty clear. A company would tell you when you could expect to hear if you got the job or not. Alas, that's not always the case.

Looking in from the outside, it seems like the process for giving you a job offer is a bit like the process for picking a new pope! You can imagine a bunch of executives sitting around a conference-room table debating your merits as a worthy employee compared to other candidates. Days, even weeks pass before you hear anything, and then suddenly the bells toll, and the white smoke appears. The company announces, "All hail! We have selected our new systems analyst!"

Shocking Sealing-the-Deal Confession #1
Some companies have completely nebulous hiring procedures.

I know many stories of candidates who interview and then never hear from the company again. Ever! Not a letter, not a phone call, and no response to any correspondence. I'm guessing that's a way of saying you didn't get the job. There are a few reasons for this, none of which I condone, by the way. The first reason is simply that the company feels it is too busy to get back to you, and by not hearing you'll assume you didn't get the job. The second is that maybe there isn't a job available any longer. Perhaps someone else took it internally, or perhaps funding for the position evaporated. Finally, there may have never been an actual opening in the first place, and the company was just interviewing you in case a position was to open up in the near future.

Now don't get frightened. Most companies don't act this way, and most companies will contact you following the interview. However, it's not always clear when and how.

Shocking Sealing-the-Deal Confession #2
You should never leave an interview without understanding the next steps.

At the end of every interview you must ask either the last person you interview with or your HR contact when you can expect to hear back from the company. It's a perfectly legitimate question. Hopefully you'll get a response like "We're seeing a few candidates and will probably know in the next four weeks." In that case you say, "Should I contact you, or will you plan to contact me?" That's pretty simple to deal with.

A bit trickier is when a company says, "Well, we're not exactly sure when we will be hiring someone." Nevertheless, you need to force the issue. You should ask, "When would be a good time for me to check in then?"

In either scenario you're looking for a date. It could be one day; it could be six weeks. But once you know the date, you then have a plan of attack.

If that date rolls around and you haven't yet heard, it's an open invitation to contact the company and check on your status. Don't worry, you won't be a bother if you simply call the recruiting director and say, "Hi, this is Doug Neuman and I interviewed last week for the systems analyst job. You indicated you'd get back to me by the twenty-first to let me know about your decision."

In a perfect world, they'd say, "Oh, we just made our decision today, and we'd like to offer you the position." However, as you well know now, nothing comes that easy in the real world.

In all likelihood you won't even reach the recruiting director in person. In fact, the single most difficult part of the job search may indeed be trying to track down this elusive figure. You want to be vigilant in trying to reach your contact, but you don't want to go overboard.

Shocking Sealing-the-Deal Confession #3
There's a fine line between persistent and stalker.

If you call the recruiting director and get his voice mail, hang up before you leave a message. Call back a couple of hours later, and if you get voice mail again, leave a message. There's this crazy little invention you may have heard of called caller ID, so you don't want to call every three minutes and then hang up when you get the machine!

The message you leave can be short and sweet, just like what you'd say if you talked to him in person. "Hi, this is Doug Neuman and I interviewed last week for the systems analyst job. You indicated you'd get back to me by the twenty-first to let me know about your decision. I'm hoping to hear from you soon. You can reach me at 617-945-3161." Always leave your phone number, even if you know the recruiting director has your number and even if you've left it dozens of times before.

If you get no response, call again in three days. Again, if you get voice mail the first time, hang up and try again a bit later. A good technique is to try to call him about fifteen to thirty minutes before the normal workday starts. If he happens to be someone who gets in early, he may be more apt to be at his desk and pick up the phone since the office may not be as hectic. If you call before work hours the first time, make sure the second time you call is during the normal workday.

After the second call, wait three more days, and then send an e-mail. It's always best to hit him with a multimedia attack! Keep the message short and sweet, just like the voice mail. In the subject line, make sure to mention your name so the recruiting director doesn't think it's spam: SUBJECT: Doug Neuman Checking In.

If you *still* don't hear anything, keep alternating between e-mail and voice mail. If you've hit him up about four times and still have nothing, try to contact other people you may have interviewed with.

In the back of your mind, though, the following question should be going through your brain: "Do I really want to work for a company that doesn't have the common decency to get back to me? What's it going to be like to work there full-time?"

Ultimately the decision is yours. How many calls will you make? How long will you wait to hear? On the one hand, all the waiting and all the phone calls could result in a job, but on the other hand, what kind of job will it be? I suggest six strikes and you're out! After six contacts with the company, call it a day and move on.

Enough with the bad stuff. It's offer time! It may be hard to believe now, but there are companies out there that will be dying to hire you. At some point you're going to get the call that says, "Congratulations, Doug, we'd like to offer you a job." Now if you're like ninety-nine out of one hundred students, your first reaction is to say, "I accept!" Then there's usually the awkward pause on the phone as the recruiting director says, "But I haven't even told you about the salary."

Shocking Sealing-the-Deal Confession #4
Never accept an offer on the spot.

Even if the recruiter tells you the salary and the position and the benefits—all the information—you always want to take some time to mull it over. Yes, you may be desperate. Yes, you may have been dreaming about working at Bain Consulting your entire college life. And yes, you may have been rejected from seventy-five other companies. But do *not* accept that offer on the spot!

Here's why. You need time to look at the specifics of what the offer is. You need to weigh all the benefits you may not have thought about, and you need to show it to someone who is versed in looking at offer letters. Chances are this will be the first official offer you receive.

If the recruiting director asks you what you think of the offer, or asks you if you can accept on the spot, just politely request some time to think it over. "It all sounds wonderful, and I'm so happy to receive the offer. I was hoping it would be okay to have a few days to look at everything."

Looking at everything is key. It's great to get an offer over the phone, but that's not enough.

Shocking Sealing-the-Deal Confession #5
Never accept a job without getting an offer in writing.

This is nonnegotiable. Any company you work with must give you a written offer. It's simply too risky to accept an offer without seeing it in writing. Horror stories are abundant about organizations later retracting an offer or saying, "We didn't say we'd pay you THIRTY-two thousand dollars; we said TWENTY-two thousand dollars." Don't feel like you're being rude or being difficult by asking to see the offer in writing. That's simply the way the business world operates. Preferably the offer letter will come to you in hard copy format, but e-mail can work just as well.

Once you get the offer, the fun begins! There are a host of things to consider when it comes time to make the big decision.

Shocking Sealing-the-Deal Confession #6
Evaluating an offer is not just evaluating the salary.

This is the single biggest mistake students make when they decide on a job. Of course your first reaction when you get an offer is "Show me the money!" And yes, it sure is cool to talk to your buddies and say, "I'm making forty-five thousand dollars. What are you making?" But the money is just the proverbial tip of the iceberg. Here's a list of all types of benefits that may accompany your salary:

- Signing bonus
- Relocation allowance
- Year-end bonus
- 401(k)
- Profit sharing
- Medical/Dental benefits
- Vacation time
- Holidays
- Summer hours
- Sick days
- Personal days
- Company perks

Didn't think about all those things, did you? In fact, you probably don't even know what some of those things are! Let's quickly define them.

SIGNING BONUS

Just like your favorite pro athlete, you may be offered a bonus for accepting some companies' work offers. Unlike your favorite pro athlete, you will likely receive an offer in the thousands and not in the millions. If you don't get a signing bonus, don't fret. Very few companies offer them. It's a leftover from the good old dot-com days!

RELOCATION ALLOWANCE

Think signing bonus with a different name. Again, it's not all too common, but some companies may help you with your move to a new city. Similarly, in a job where you might need a new wardrobe, they may give you an allowance for clothing.

YEAR-END BONUS

Typically a discretionary bonus based on how the company performs, or how you perform, or both, these can range anywhere from five hundred dollars to 30 percent of your salary. In all honesty, though, it's a rare perk.

401(K)

This is a retirement savings plan. You may have heard of an IRA. It's very similar. I know retirement is a long ways away, but these programs are important for your future. (I sound like your father now!) The way it works is this: You put away a certain amount of money each paycheck for your retirement *before* you pay taxes on it (the amount you sock away can be just a few bucks), and the company will match a portion of what you put away. (In other words, this company match is free money.) Most companies match around 3 to 5 percent of your base salary.

PROFIT SHARING

Profit sharing can take different forms. At some companies, it's a supercharged 401(k) plan. It works the same as a 401(k), except the company puts in all the money and you don't put in a cent! At other companies profit sharing can mean company stock or other bonuses. We like companies that offer profit sharing.

MEDICAL/DENTAL BENEFITS

We could write an entire book on these. Basically, most companies offer medical insurance for full-time employees. Sometimes you're responsible for picking the plan, and sometimes the company does it for you. In essence you usually have the chance to choose your deductible, the certain doctors you can see, your copayment for each office visit, and your maximum payment in the event of an emergency. Usually the company pays a portion of your monthly insurance premium and you pay the rest. Depending on the coverage and the company, that payment can be anywhere from zero to three hundred dollars a month.

VACATION TIME

Your first slap in the face in the real world. Most companies provide two weeks of paid vacation. In college you get about fifteen weeks of vacation a year among summer, winter, and spring breaks. The party is officially now over. The good news about the two weeks is that it's usually paid vacation. That means you're making money when you're sitting on the beach in Cancun! Generous companies may provide three or more weeks, and some companies may start you with a week your first year of work. But the overriding vacation policy for new hires is two weeks of paid vacation.

HOLIDAYS

Most companies offer the standard ten or so paid holidays a year. If you're lucky, some may offer a few more, or even "floating holidays" to use as you wish (e.g., "I declare November 21—my birthday—as a holiday.").

SUMMER HOURS

This is a growing trend in which companies close down at 1:00 p.m. on Friday during the summers in exchange for working an extra hour Monday through Thursday. There are a few variations on the theme, but it helps extend the precious summer weekends for sun-starved Northerners!

SICK DAYS/PERSONAL DAYS

Some organizations offer unlimited personal or sick days and others offer just a set amount. This can be an important benefit. If a company provides five sick days a year and you end up being sick for eight days, you have to take three vacation days or you get docked pay. Personal days are days out of the office for things like funerals, jury duty, moving, or other "emergencies."

COMPANY PERKS

These can range anywhere from absolutely nothing to benefits far and wide. Typically these perks aren't usually the difference makers when choosing a job, but they can end up playing a big role in your overall happiness. Again, most companies may not offer much in this area, and others will offer a host of benefits. These can include tuition reimbursement for classes you take or graduate degrees, student-loan assistance programs, casual dress in the office place, free soda/coffee, discounted/free health club memberships, corporate matching for charitable donations, free lunch in the company cafeteria, bring your pet to work day . . . the list can go on and on.

Phew! There sure is a lot to consider when looking at an offer. For those of you in the enviable position of having multiple offers, you need to weigh all the benefits, not just salary. For instance, if Company A offers full medical benefits with no monthly premium copayment, while Company B makes you pay $200 a month, the difference is $2,400 a year. That's a lot of money! The same goes for tuition reimbursement. If you know you want to go to grad school to get your MBA at night, and one company will pay for that, it could mean up to $10,000 a year!

The best thing to do if you are evaluating multiple offers is to lay out all the benefits on a sheet of paper and see how the two companies measure up.

Let's take a look:

BENEFIT	COMPANY A	COMPANY B
Salary:	$36,000	$30,000
Vacation:	2 Weeks	3 Weeks
Bonus:	0	10% based on performance
401(k):	No match	4% match
Monthly Medical:	$100	$25
Summer Hours:	No	Yes
Perks:	None	Free Health Club

In just considering salary, you'd have to go with Company A. But obviously when you lay out the offer, you see that Company B is much better. Even if you look at the money, a 10 percent bonus translates into

$3,000, a 4% 401(k) match equals $1,200 a year, and $75 a month less in health-care premiums means $900 a year in your pocket. That totals $5,100 in yearly benefits. So suddenly a $6,000 difference in salary is really only $900 a year! And I don't know about you, but an extra week of vacation, summer hours, and a free health club are worth at least $900 a year to me.

Of course the most important benefit isn't even listed above.

Shocking Sealing-the-Deal Confession #7
Your overall happiness on the job is the most important determining factor.

I've worked with many students who make a job decision based on a few bucks in salary. They'll say, "Sure, I like Company X better, but Company Y is offering me $2,000 more a year in salary and benefits. Maybe I'll do the job for a year or two and make some extra cash."

Let's look at how much "cash" that means. Most organizations pay you twice a month, which means you get paid twenty-four times a year. After Uncle Sam gets his share, that $2,000 translates to about $62.50 a pay period. I think you'd agree that sixty-two bucks, twice a month, is not worth your overall happiness!

The final piece of the "Sealing the Deal" puzzle is negotiating your offer.

Shocking Sealing-the-Deal Confession #8
You have virtually no leverage when it comes to negotiating.

I hate to be the bearer of bad news on this one, but it's not like some other recent college graduates you may have read about:

"Star quarterback vows to sit out season unless salary demand of $4,000,000 a year is met."

Somehow I just can't imagine the following headline in the newspapers.

"Star accounting student vows to sit out tax season unless salary demand of $50,000 is met."

Especially at a large company that's hiring lots of new grads, you really have no ability to negotiate. Starting salaries are typically set in stone, and benefits are standard for all employees. That being said, if you'd like to take a shot at negotiating, you can. But be careful!

Shocking Sealing-the-Deal Confession #9
You get one and only one chance to negotiate.

It's perfectly acceptable to politely and professionally ask if there is a way to negotiate your offer. Notice I didn't say negotiating your salary. Hopefully we just learned that you need to consider more than your salary when looking at a job offer. In fact, you're more likely to find negotiating room in some of the benefits beyond salary—things like vacation time, signing bonus, or tuition reimbursement. Remember, especially for your first job, you need to have a reason to negotiate. Negotiating for the pure sake of just getting more money is usually not worth it. So do your homework.

Check out salary surveys in trade publications, through the US Department of Labor Statistics, and on job sites like Monster and Yahoo!. They'll tell you what typical starting salaries are in your field and in your city. Of course, it's also easier to negotiate if you have another offer somewhere. Here are some negotiating scenarios:

"Based on research I did, I discovered that the range of salaries for entry-level accountants in Dallas is $35,000–$45,000 and since my offer is for $32,000 I was hoping to be able to make a salary within that range."

"In order to accept this job, I'll have to move from Cleveland to Los Angeles, and I was wondering if your company offers any type of relocation allowance."

"I would absolutely love to accept your offer, and your company is my first choice, but I do have another offer that pays $3,000 more. If you would be able to match that salary, I would accept your offer right now."

These are all perfectly legitimate ways to negotiate, but all more than likely to be met with a resounding no! Again, larger companies especially do not negotiate offers. You may have more leeway with smaller organizations where they don't necessarily have "rules" already in place.

If you are met with a no, then absolutely stop the negotiating there.

Shocking Sealing-the-Deal Confession #10
You can ruin your reputation by overnegotiating.

We gave an offer to a new college grad at my former company, and she tried to negotiate again and again and again. She told us she had more experience due to her internships, was a better candidate since she came from a better school, and would contribute more from day one. None of those facts were true. When we told her we didn't negotiate salary, she asked for free airplane tickets, free personal technology devices, and extra benefits. She engaged in repeated conversations with three separate people at the company before she reluctantly stopped asking for more. We seriously considered rescinding her offer, and in retrospect, I wish we had.

The fallout was that her reputation was tarnished before she even came into the company. She was perceived to be a malcontent and ultimately didn't do well or last long on the job.

The bottom line is that you should think about your first job as an investment in your career. Yes, you want to make good money. Yes, you want to have great benefits. But ultimately you want to be happy, you want to learn, and you want to grow. If that means you lose out on an extra $62 a paycheck, so be it!

Once you've worked for a company for six months to a year, and established yourself as a true talent and a valuable contributor, it's much easier to ask for a raise or for a promotion than it is at the get-go.

Finding out if you even have an offer and then deciding whether or not to accept it can be tricky business. But now that you know how the system works from the inside, you can navigate and negotiate your way to success.

SEVEN

Conclusion— No More Shocking Confessions; It's Time to Get a Job

So there you have it. The insider's guide to landing your first job: sixty-two shocking confessions that will forever change the way you think about getting a job. If you've read through this entire book, I'm sure you've been amazed at how the job-hiring process works. It's quite astonishing to see it from the inside out—from the perspective of a recruiting director.

It's part science and it's part art. To be sure, it can be very arbitrary. I knew that when I was a recruiting director and I received five hundred resumes for one job, there were dozens of people who *could* do the job. The problem was I didn't know exactly which ones, and I could only hire one of them!

If you think about how the game is played, it's all about putting yourself in the right position to win. There's no surefire, quick, and easy way to get a job. You just have to make sure you do the right thing throughout the entire process. You need to

- Network your way into as many companies as possible
- Have an accomplishment-laden resume that will pass the fifteen-second test

- Write an amazing cover letter that tells your unique story
- Prepare for an interview and be relaxed, confident, and persuasive
- Write a thank-you note that will summarize your interest in the company
- Follow up and negotiate with equal parts politeness and persistence

Nobody said it would be easy, and nobody said it would be fun. Some folks claim that getting a job is a full-time job in and of itself. Now I don't think it takes forty hours a week, but it does take dedicated time and effort. The fact is you have to get out and do it, so you might as well know as much inside information as you can. It makes the process go infinitely smoother. You want to approach the process by working smarter, not just working harder.

Now that you know the inner workings of the recruiting process, now that you know how recruiting directors think, and now that you know how companies hire people, you'll definitely have the edge when it comes to getting that dream job.

Good luck!

Appendix

Every good job-search book has a sampling of resumes at the end of the book. But *Confessions of a Recruiting Director* does it a bit differently. First of all, you'll see that the resumes written here are simply better than the ones you've seen before. That's because they were all rewritten by former recruiting directors who know exactly what it takes to write the perfect resume. You'll also notice that the resumes are very specific and personal to the individual. Much as I know you'd like to take some of these resumes and simply insert your own information, it's not going to work.

By definition a well-written resume is going to be unique.

That being said, you'll certainly get a great sense of *how* to write your resume based on what you've seen and based on the information in the rest of the book.

The biggest difference in this book is that we have *before and after* resumes. You will simply be amazed by how much better the after versions are. Many students think their resumes are pretty good, but are then blown away when they see how good their resumes can be. Take some time to look, really look, at the before and after versions. See how a candidate comes to life. See how accomplishments make a resume sound so much better than job descriptions. And see why recruiting directors crave the after versions.

Importantly, every single resume example in the book is an actual student before resume and an actual student after resume as written by Job-Bound. Of course, all the vital information has been changed, but these are real student resumes. I promise you, your resume before reading this book looks very similar to a before version.

Imagine, as you read these resumes that you are a recruiting director. Do the before versions tell you much about a candidate? Do they paint a clear picture of what the candidate has accomplished? Would you select a before resume from a stack of 500? Then look at the after versions. They tell you so much more about a candidate, what they've accomplished, and why they would do well in the real world. It's like a breath of fresh air!

We've also included cover letters. Since virtually every student cover letter is written the same way, and since we showed a before version in the cover letter chapter, we're just putting after cover letters in the appendix.

We've grouped the resumes alphabetically by field. Not every field is represented, but don't worry. It's more about the concept of making the best of what you've done as opposed to finding the perfect resume for your field. You'll discover information you can use from a marketing resume, even if you want to become a botanist.

For the cover letters, they are sorted according to "story," in other words what the candidates are trying to tell the recruiting director about themselves. These letters will help inspire you to determine what your story is for your cover letter.

Remember, it's not about copying what you see on the following pages; it's about getting a sense of the thought behind resumes and cover letters and applying that to your specific situation.

Go get 'em!

Sample Resumés

BEFORE: ACCOUNTING

2000 Myoctopus Street
Central, CA 82982

Taryn Twarner

Objective

To obtain an auditing position with a public accounting firm.

Education

August 2003-Present   **University of California, Santa Barbara**   Santa Barbara, CA
Expected Graduation   June 2007
B.A., Business/Economics with an emphasis in accounting
Minor, Sports Management.
Minor, Athletic Coaching
Accounting GPA 3.35

Experience

June 2005-August 2006   **UCSB Finance Department**   Santa Barbara, CA
Finance Internship
Assisted in the preparation of year-end audit materials and closing procedures for Alumni
    programming.
Assisted with the projection of annual budgets for current and next fiscal years.
Reconciled monthly bank statements of several accounts managing up to two million dollars.
Attended quarterly Board of Directors, Finance Committee meetings.
Prepared the minutes, investment reports and various financial sections of the Finance Board book

February 2005–February 2006   **Flynn Embroidery, LLC**   Santa Barbara, CA
Bookkeeper/ Office Manager
Managed accounts payables, receivables, payroll, tax, reconciliation and account processing.
Influenced and assisted with the modifications of current invoices and proposals in Microsoft
    Access to minimize invoicing errors.
Implemented automated monthly sales tax payment system.
Developed several Excel spreadsheet macros currently in use for reducing entry time and
    automatically cross-referencing for errors.

August 2005-February 2005   **Goleta National Bank**   Santa Barbara, CA
Teller
Administered sensitive accounts with ITI data system.
Balanced cash drawers, money orders, cashier checks, and vault.

Activities

March 2005- Present   **Accounting Association**
* Active Member

August 2005-Present   **Gamma Phi Beta Sorority**
Membership Vice President, February 2004-Present
Public Relations Vice President, February 2003-February 2004

continues on next page . . .

September 2003-Present   **UCSB Panhellenic Council**
Programming Coordinator, April 2005-January 2006
Risk Management, January 2004-January 2005

References   Available upon request.

AFTER: ACCOUNTING

Taryn Twarner

taryn@minnino.net ♦ 916.799.2449
2000 Myoctopus Street ♦ Central, CA 82982

Education
University of California–Santa Barbara: June 2007
Bachelor of Arts, Business/Economics – Accounting emphasis
Double Minor: Sports Management, Athletic Coaching
Accounting GPA: 3.4/4.0

Experience
Finance Intern, UCSB Finance Department, June '05 – August '06
- Worked closely with the management of six departments to help project more than $2MM in annual budgets
- Rectified more than $75,000 in accounting mistakes by reconciling dozens of monthly bank statements
- Presented audit findings to CFO at quarterly Finance Committee meetings
- Prepared investment reports, meeting minutes, and several financial sections of Finance Board book presented to university Board of Directors
- Helped prepare year-end audit materials and closing procedures for alumni programming
- Worked full time in summers and 15 – 20 hours/week during school year while maintaining full course load

Bookkeeper/Office Manager, Flynn Embroidery, Santa Barbara, CA, February '05 – February '06
- Reduced invoicing errors 15% by helping execute migration to Microsoft Access invoicing system
- Overhauled and implemented new automated monthly sales tax payment system
- Introduced company's first computerized system to back up all accounting files
- Managed $80,000 in monthly accounts receivable and payable across hundreds of vendors and customers
- Processed all year-end closing procedures to balance out 2005
- Executed payroll, tax, reconciliation, and account processing
- Worked 10 hours/week while maintaining full course load and internship

Vice President Membership, Gamma Phi Beta Sorority, February '06 – Present
- Exceeded previous spring's recruitment totals by successfully filling house quota
- Revamped weeklong recruitment process for more than 400 women by reorganizing internal structure
- Oversee a staff of 20 membership team personnel
- Introduced new initiate workshop, helping 37 members improve recruiting skills

Teller, Goleta National Bank, Santa Barbara, CA, August '05 – February '05
- Administered key $500,000 – $1,000,000 sensitive accounts with ITI data system
- Balanced more than $10,000/day in cash drawers, money orders, cashier checks, and vault
- Caught consumer "kiting" funds between two accounts

Activities/Interests
- Accounting Association, Member, 2005 – Present
- VIDA, IRS Volunteer, prepared taxes for low-income families, 2004
- American Cancer Society Relay for Life, Volunteer, 2006
- UCSB Panhellenic Council, Programming Coordinator/Risk Management, 2004–2006
- Interests include volleyball, snowboarding, and comedy shows

BEFORE: ADVERTISING

Lance Lot

Objective

- Join an established, forward-thinking ad agency in an account coordinating position.

Experience

01/06-06/06   *Southwest Missouri State University Advertising Team*   *Springfield, MO*
Media Director, Plansbook Writer, Marketing Researcher
Selected one of seventeen people to the team
Strategic planner & writer of plansbook
Researched activities including data collection, secret shopping, & personal interviews
Coproduced promotional activities
Planned, placed, & implemented media selections
Coordinated budget estimation & allocation

01/05-05/05   *Wilks Broadcasting, Inc.*   *Springfield, MO*
Advertising & Marketing Intern
Maintained advertising accounts' traffic scheduling
Helped produce advertisements including script writing & voice-overs
Successfully promoted & marketed concert events

06/03-Present   *Wal-Mart Stores, Inc.*   *Springfield, MO*
Customer Courtesy Associate
Ensure excellent customer service in a fast-paced environment
Organize inventory of store merchandise
Maintained safety procedures while on store risk management team

Education

- *Southwest Missouri State University*   *Springfield, MO*
B.S. Mass Media, Journalism, & Film, Completed August 2006
B.S. Marketing with emphasis in Advertising & Promotion, Anticipated December 2007

Skills & Awards

- *Microsoft Word, Microsoft Excel, Internet, Basic Adobe Photoshop, Avid Editing Software*
- *2005 American Advertising Federation National Student Advertising Competition:*
  District 9, First Place   *Kansas City, MO*
- *American Advertising Federation Addy Advertising Award: Keep the Grey Ad*
- *Southwest Missouri State Film Festival: Misunderstood*
- *Dean's List for high academic achievement*

Activities

- *American Advertising Federation*
- *Southwest Missouri State University Advertising Team*
- *Advertising Club, Marketing Club*
- *Alpha Kappa Psi Business Fraternity*
- *Sports, outdoors, traveling, & playing guitars*

AFTER: ADVERTISING

Lance Lot
4235 S. Lifeson Avenue • Landers, MO 76918
528.993.9988 • lancelot@smsu.edu

Objective
To obtain a position in the account management department of an advertising agency

Education
Southwest Missouri State University – Springfield, MO, December 2007
B.S. Marketing (Advertising/Promotion emphasis)
B.S. Mass Media, Journalism, and Film, August 2006
Dean's List, Spring 2005

Experience
Marketing Researcher, Visit Florida, National Student Advertising Competition, Spring 2006
- Prepared $7MM fully integrated brand plan as part of nation's largest student advertising competition
- Team placed first at regional competition in Sioux City, Iowa
- Developed and executed comprehensive research plan including recruiting 120 respondents, preparing qualitative questionnaire for 12 focus groups, and coding research data

Media Director, Toyota Matrix, National Student Advertising Competition, Spring 2005
- Team placed eighth out of 150 schools at national competition in Los Angeles, California
- Helped develop $35MM marketing communications plan presented to Toyota and Saatchi & Saatchi
- Led team of three in creating media plan comprising media selection, scheduling, and budgeting across TV, print, radio, out-of-home, and online

Advertising/Marketing Intern, Wilks Broadcasting Inc., Springfield, MO, 1/05 – 5/05
- Scheduled and loaded radio commercials for 20 national and regional clients including Tylenol, Blockbuster Video, and Enterprise Rent-A-Car
- Responsible for scheduling more than 500 individual spots across all day parts
- Wrote three press releases announcing concert sponsorships distributed to the local media
- Developed promotional plans and helped with all executional elements for three area concerts
- Worked 12 hours/week while maintaining a full course load

Customer Courtesy Associate, Wal-Mart Stores Inc., Springfield, MO, 6/03 – Present
- Awarded "four-star cashier" out of more than 50 cashiers for superior performance
- Selected to serve on store's risk management team
- Work 30 hours/week during school year, and full-time throughout the summer

Activities/Interests
- Gold Student Addy Winner, 2006
- Southwest Missouri State Film Festival, Entrant, 2005
- American Advertising Federation, Member, 2006 – Present
- Marketing Club, Member, 2005 – Present
- Alpha Kappa Psi Business Fraternity, Member, 2005 – Present
- Southwest Missouri State Ad Club, 2004 – Present
- Interests include sports, traveling, hiking, photography, and the letter E

BEFORE: ADVERTISING

Brittany Beleeves

Brittanylynn@yahoo.com

Objective   To obtain an advertising position in the area of copywriting.

Education   2002-2006   **Bradley University**   Peoria, IL
B.A, Communication Advertising, Minor in Business Marketing. May 2006.
3.22 Overall GPA; 3.55 in Communication Courses

Sept 2004-Dec.2004   **Richmond University**   London, England
* Study Abroad

Work Experience   2001-Present   **J Crew**   Oak Brook, IL
Sales Associate/Cashier
Trained new associates on the registers
Assisted customers on the sales floor and on the telephone
Assisted in setting the store windows and floor displays

Leadership   2002-2006   **Bradley University**   Peoria, IL
Sigma Delta Tau Sorority
Philanthropy Day Chair
Headed a 15 person committee
Communicated ideas and opinions to my committee, executive board and
    Greek Advisor, Nathan Thomas
Sig Delt Dude Contestant Committee Head
Delegated responsibility to 20 of my committee members
Worked closely with the Presidents of 14 fraternities on campus
Organized a 2 hour pageant
Campus Awareness for Rape Education (CARE)
Classroom Presenter
Presented rape awareness presentations to Freshman Students
Worked diligently with a team of 3-4 members to educate students
    on rape education on college campuses

Skills   Skilled in and have worked with MS Word and PowerPoint. Adobe
Photoshop and PageMaker as well as Internet Explorer.

AFTER: ADVERTISING

Brittany Beleeves

72085 Zeta Avenue • Centenary, TX 70739
419.573.7919 • brittanylynn@yahoo.com

Education
Bradley University – Peoria, IL: May 2006
Bachelor of Arts in Communication Advertising
Business Marketing Minor
Major GPA 3.6/4.0, Overall GPA 3.2/4.0
Dean's List, Spring 2005

Richmond University – London, England: Fall 2004
Studied business writing, psychology, and photography as part of semester abroad

Experience
Chairman – Philanthropy Day, Sigma Delta Tau Sorority, Fall 2005
- Selected to lead team of 15 in planning and executing philanthropy effort for 600 participants
- Contributed to one of the highest retention rates and best recruitment years in sorority's history
- Created event theme and handled all planning logistics

Sales Associate, J Crew, Oak Brook, IL, Summers 2001 – 2005
- Ranked #1 in sales out of 20 other associates for three separate months
- Won employee of the month three times for going above and beyond normal requirements
- Collected, verified, and deposited more than $18,000 in cash and checks monthly
- Requested by manager to work during all school breaks

Classroom Presenter, Campus Awareness for Rape Education, 2004 – 2005
- Selected as one of 20 presenters out of a campus of 6,000
- Presented rape awareness programs to more than 350 freshman students

Committee Head, Prevent Child Abuse America, Spring 2006
- Raised more than $10,000, exceeding previous year's total by 250%
- Reorganized weeklong event introducing new programs and spearheading increased fund-raising
- Selected to lead team of 20 in executing campuswide event

Activities/Interests
- Bradley University Ad Club, Member, 2003
- Activities Council Bradley University, Member, 2003 – 2004
- Habitat for Humanity, Volunteer, 2005
- Children's Miracle Network, Volunteer, 2003 – 2006
- Intramural Volleyball, Soccer, 2003 – 2006
- Interests include photography, dancing, travel, outdoor activities, and tabloid magazines

BEFORE: BANKING

Present Address	Harper Hulmer	Permanent Address
8181 W. Harrison,	hulmer@su.edu	51 W 979 Hanly Dr.
Hilltop, TN 61801		Elgin, TN 71234
Phone: (328) 495-6759		**Phone:** (958) 575-6999
(958) 944-3359		

OBJECTIVE	To obtain an internship in the financial services industry, integrating technical skills and business knowledge, to allow for personal and professional growth.

EDUCATION

Sanders University - Memphis, TN
College of Business
Bachelor of Science in Finance, May 2006
Concentrations/Minor: Accounting
GPA: 3.89/4.0

Burlington Central High School – Burlington, TN   1999-2003
GPA: 4.29/4.0
Class Rank: 3/156
ACT Score: 32

WORK EXPERIENCE

Fox Valley Blues – McHenry, TN   Summer 2004
Umpire-Softball & Baseball
- Mentored junior high school boys team
- Acquired exceptional mediation skills
- Obtained an understanding of positions with decision making responsibilities
- Acquired leadership skills by being held accountable of the field
- Taught children fundamentals and rules of softball and baseball

Alright Concrete – Streamwood, TN   Summer 2003
Manual Labor
- Attained exceptional teamwork skills due to fast paced work environment
- Learned to communicate with people of different backgrounds and languages
- Obtained an incomparable work ethic via a rigorous work schedule

HONORS & ACTIVITIES

- Pi Kappa Alpha Social Fraternity
- Saint Josephs Hospital
- Times Homeless Shelter
- National Society of Collegiate Scholars
- Lockhart Scholar
- Enjoy softball, golf and basketball

COMPUTER SKILLS   Visual Basic, MS-Office and SQL

REFERENCES AVAILABLE UPON REQUEST

AFTER: BANKING

Harper Hulmer
hulmer@su.edu
958.944.3359

Campus	**Permanent**
818 West Harrison	**51 West 979 Hanly Dr.**
Hilltop, TN 61801	**Elgin, TN 71234**

Education
Sanders University – Memphis, TN: May 2006
- Bachelor of Science in Finance, Accounting Minor
- College of Business
- Overall GPA 3.9/4.0
- Lockhart Scholar – awarded based on superior academic achievement
- Dean's List all semesters

Experience
Financial Representative Intern, Northwestern Mutual, Skokie, TN, Summer 2005
- Ranked first out of five interns, writing more than $10,000 in annual life insurance premiums
- Secured 10 clients in two months with a close rate of 25%
- Worked in same capacity as full-time staff, both soliciting clients and selling products
- Developed complete financial analyses for 25 actual and potential clients covering investment, savings, and retirement strategies
- Created customer-centric contact plans for core group of potential clients
- Internship recognized as "Top Ten Internships You Can Have" by the *Princeton Review*

President/Founder, Tennessee Investors, Fall 2004 – Present
- Manage a member-funded portfolio of more than $10,000
- Grew club from founding members to more than 20 by introducing a new recruiting process
- Oversee 10 biweekly presentations to help determine club investment strategies
- Developed bylaws and constitution, and secured official university recognition
- Focus organization on equity research, valuation, and investments

Umpire, Fox Valley Blues, McHenry, TN, Summer 2004
- Selected to officiate for Tennessee's leading umpire association
- Chosen as youngest person out of 175 to umpire a varsity game at age of 17
- Travel to Nashville area to work 10+ hours per week in spring and fall while managing a full course load

Activities/Interests
- Finance Club, member, 2004 – Present
- National Society of Collegiate Scholars, member, 2004 – Present
- Pi Kappa Alpha, member, 2003 – Present
- Proficient in Visual Basic and SQL
- Interests include softball, golf, and reading political satire books

BEFORE: BIOLOGIST

1005 DALE STREET • MALVIN, MS 83100
PHONE: (712) 421-8511 • FAX: (712) 377-3631 • E-MAIL: WALZATO@AOL.COM

Richard Rike

Education

8/03-12/07   University of Southern Mississippi   Hattiesburg, MS
Bachelors of Science in Biological Science with a Chemistry Minor

Professional experience

Internship under Dr. Candace Collins, M.D. (2005-2006)

Biology Lab Teacher's Assistant (2005-2006)

Crescent City Grill Server (2004-2006)

Extracurricular activities

Alpha Tau Omega Fraternity (2003-2007)
President (2006)
Vice President (2005)
Secretary (2004)
Philanthropy Chair (2003)

Future Optometrists of America (2006)
Charter Member (2006)

Inter-Fraternity Council (2004-2006)
Vice President of Philanthropy (2005)

Catholic Student Association (2003-2006)

Student Government Association (2003-2004)
Freshman Associates (2003-2004)

Southern Miss Orientation Director (2004-2005)

Fraternity Recruitment Counselor (2004,2005)

Awards received

Dean's List (2005, 2006)

Alpha Epsilon Delta Honor Society (2006)

Omicron Delta Kappa Honor Society (2006)
Order of Omega Honor Society (2004-2006)

Gamma Sigma Alpha Honor Society (2006)

continues on next page . . .

References

References upon request

AFTER: BIOLOGIST

Richard Rike

1005 Dale Street • Malvin, MS 83100
712.421.8511 • richard@aol.com

Education

University of Southern Mississippi – Hattiesburg, December 2007
- Bachelor of Science in Biological Sciences, Chemistry Minor
- Alpha Epsilon Delta Honor Society – premed honor society based on GPA
- Omicron Delta Kappa Honor Society – nominated by faculty for outstanding campus leadership
- Order of Omega Honor Society – awarded to 100 students out of 4000 for academics and leadership
- Gamma Sigma Alpha Honor Society – based on high scholastic achievement
- Dean's List, 2005 – Present

Experience

Ophthalmology Intern, Dr. Candice Collins, MD, Slidell, LA, May 2006 – Present
- Transcribed 20 patient charts discussing medication and vision prescriptions
- Observed 100 appointments for issues including glaucoma, macular degeneration, and detached retinas
- Helped fit new contact lens patients

Biology Lab Teaching Assistant, University of Southern Mississippi, August 2005 – June 2006
- Independently taught two biology labs per semester with 20 students in each
- Created lesson plans and modified and presented curriculum for weekly classes
- Maintained lab with spiders, guinea pigs, beetles, and gecko
- Held weekly office hours and tutored dozens of students

President, Alpha Tau Omega Fraternity, November 2005 – November 2006
- Improved house academic standing from tenth to first on campus by instituting new scholarship program
- Increased philanthropic giving 66% to $50,000 annually by overhauling two campuswide fund-raisers
- Ranked first out of 140 ATO national chapters in total philanthropic hours donated
- One of 28 chapters in the country to win ATO True Merit Award for overall excellence across scholarship, philanthropy, communications, and operations

Founding Member, Future Optometrists of America, USM, Spring 2006 – Present
- Helped create USM's first chapter of national student organization
- Petitioned and secured official club status from student government
- Wrote constitution, bylaws, and mission statement and established executive structure

Vice President of Philanthropy, Inter-Fraternity Council, Fall 2004 – Spring 2005
- Organized pan-Greek Habitat for Humanity event attended by 250 students
- Tracked monthly philanthropic hours and dollars raised for entire fraternity population

Activities/Interests
- USM Orientation Director, 2004 – 2006
- Student Government Association, Freshman Associate, 2003 – 2004
- Catholic Student Association, Member, 2003 – Present
- Alpha Tau Omega, Member, 2003 – Present
- Intramural football, softball, basketball, soccer, 2003 – Present
- Interests include music, sports, travel, volunteering, and James Michener novels

BEFORE: BROADCAST JOURNALIST

Quentina Quagmire

713 E. ORANGE STREET, APT 519	PHONE (819) 749-3278
CHACKBAY, OK 72931	E-MAIL QUAGMIRE@OK.EDU

Objective
To obtain an on-air position with WIHN, 96.7 The Rock.

Education

[8/99 – 6/03]   Victor J. Andrew High School   Arlington, OK
[8/03 – present]   University of Oklahoma   Chackbay, OK
Broadcast Journalism
- Senior Standing in the College of Communications, Broadcast Journalism Curriculum, Interdisciplinary Minor in Gender and Women's Studies

[8/04 – present]   Cochrane On Daniel's   Chackbay, OK

Work experience

Head Bartender [4/05 – present]
Responsible for customer service and maintenance of the establishment.
Oversee staff members.
Train new staff members.
Party Booker [8/06 – present]
Plan and book social events.
[4/05 – present]   WPGU – 107.1 The Planet   Chackbay, OK
Promotional Director [4/05 – present]
Plan and run all station promotional events.
Develop on-air promotional ideas.
Develop Promotions Department intern program.
Maintain high level of communication with Programming, Production, Sales, Marketing, Advertising, and full-time staff.
Develop new station image and relaunch agenda.
On-Air Personality Middays [4/05 – present]
Develop listener interactive show concepts.
Serve as an on-air talent.
[2/02 – 6/02]   WILL – TV   Urbana, OK
Volunteer
Run studio cameras.
Floor directing.

Extracurricular activities
Alpha Chi Omega Sorority – Vice President Chapter Relations and Standards

•Responsible for annual revision of chapter governing documents

•Responsible for discipline and regulation of all chapter members

University of Oklahoma Panhellenic Council 2006 Recruitment

continues on next page . . .

Counselor
Mayor's Midnight Sun Marathon – Anchorage, AK, June 22, 2004.
The LaSalle Bank Chicago Marathon – Chicago, IL, October 12, 2005.
Alpha Lambda Delta Honor Society

Honors

Phi Eta Sigma Honor Society

AFTER: BROADCAST JOURNALIST

Quentina Quagmire
713 E. Orange Street, Apt. 519 • Chackbay, OK 72931
819.749.3278 • quagmire@ok.edu

Education
University of Oklahoma – Norman, May 2007
Bachelor of Arts in Broadcast Journalism, Interdisciplinary Minor in Gender and Women's Studies
Phi Eta Sigma Honor Society, membership based on superior academics
Alpha Lambda Delta Honor Society, for outstanding GPA

Experience
Promotions Director, WPGU 107.1FM, Chackbay, OK, April 2005 – Present
- Revamped remote broadcast process overhauling on-site logistics and improving client experience for up to 20 remotes per month
- Relaunched station including format change, rebranding, image reinvigoration, and created "street team" to canvas local area, as part of 15-person executive committee
- Oversee integrated promotional programs for clients including FedEx, Budweiser, and Hardee's
- Created new client evaluation and promotional staff evaluation forms insuring overall quality and driving dramatically improved event execution
- Plan and execute "PGU Pre-game" tailgate party – station's largest event attended by more than 300 students and staffed by 75 station employees
- Launched department's internship program, enhancing training, evaluations, and work content for 20 interns
- Manage a staff of 20 for a 3,000-watt station covering 50 miles and targeting 70,000 18 – 34-year-olds
- Work 35 – 40 hours/week while maintaining a full course load

On-Air Personality, WPGU 107.1FM, Chackbay, OK, April 2005 – Present
- Promoted to host Monday – Friday 9:00 a.m. to noon slot
- Handle weather, news reads, and listener calls
- Created a host of programs including *American Idol* spoof, guilty music pleasures, and rock star crush

Event Planner/Head Bartender, Cochrane On Daniel's, Chackbay, OK, April 2005 – Present
- Partnered with six social committee chairs to sell and plan several key bar events
- Oversaw a total staff of 50 student bartenders: 12 – 15/night
- Trained more than 50 new staff members, bartenders, and servers

Vice President – Chapter Relations/Standards, Alpha Chi Omega Sorority, Fall 2005 – Fall 2006
- Led house finances from deficit to surplus by rewriting bylaws and overhauling financial operations
- Developed new house rules governing all activities for chapter with 155 members and 55 live-ins
- Chapter nominated as most improved out of 27 sororities on campus

Activities/Interests
- American Cancer Society, Relay for Life participant, 2005 – 2006
- OK Union Board Spring Musical, 2005
- Leukemia Team in Training, Mayor's Midnight Sun Marathon Runner, Anchorage, AK, 2004
- LaSalle Bank Chicago Marathon Runner, 2005
- Panhellenic Council Recruitment Counselor, 2006
- Interests include running, fitness, dancing, astrology

BEFORE: BUSINESS ADMINISTRATION

Chris Clark

57 Corvette Drive
Carson, CO 71121
Home Phone: (958)493-4315
Cellular Phone: (884) 999-9498

OBJECTIVE
I am looking for an entry to mid-level position, which entails displaying strong leadership, communication; and interpersonal skills. These are skills that I have obtained through past employment experience and education. I function well under stressful conditions, and always go far above and beyond what is expected of myself or my position. I enjoy working with people, products; and organizational management.

QUALIFICATIONS
*   Thorough Knowledge Department of Health and Human Services (CMS, CDC, NIOSH, OPHS, HRSA, NIH, FDA, SAMHSA, ATSDR) as well as OSHA, HIPAA, FMLA, MSA's, HIPC's
*   Thorough understanding of Marketing, Operations Management, Finance, Accounting, Business Statistics and Economics
*   Knowledge of -Java programming
*   Languages spoken- English, Spanish, Hindi, Punjabi
*   Languages written- English, Spanish

EDUCATION
> 2005-present- **Master of Public Health, Benedictine University**
> > Coursework (75% complete thus far) towards a Master's Degree in
> > Public Health concentrating in **Health Care Administration**
> > *   **Grade Point Average= 3.8/4.0**

> 2004 B.A.- Marketing, Loyola University Chicago
> > **Was among the 1/2 of 1 percent of the nation's college students nominated to the National Dean's List**

CAREER RELATED EMPLOYMENT
> 2003   **Leo Burnett, USA,** Chicago, IL   <u>Account Management Intern</u>
> > **Was one of nine people selected for the account management internship out of a pool of 4,000 plus applicants.** Gained hands-on experience in advertising. Worked on the Allstate advertising campaign, and performed an in-depth research study on marketing and operation strategies dealing with e-commerce. Also performed in-depth market research on specific, potential target markets.

> 2002   **Fidelity Investments,** Schaumburg, IL **Financial Representative Intern**
> > Aided the investor office in daily activities needed to efficiently operate the business. Responsible for updating and ordering prospectuses, arranging appointments, portfolio allocation, answering customer questions and inquiries; check processing and assisting in the establishment of new accounts and processing of deposits.

OTHER EMPLOYMENT
> 2004   **Americorps NCCC**, Charleston, SC
> > Was among the 20% selected to perform community service in areas such as education, health, environment, and unmet human needs.

continues on next page . . .

AFFILIATIONS/ORGANIZATIONS

- Delta Sigma Pi-member 2001-2004; vice president of professional operations 2004
- Habitat for Humanities-volunteer
- American Red Cross-disaster relief specialist
- CPR & First Aid Certified

REFERENCES (contact information available upon request)

- Lisa Ulisno- Leo Burnett, USA
- Antoineete DuRoss- Americorps NCCC
- Willis Kelly- Fidelity Investments
- Brian Browned- Benedictine University

AFTER: BUSINESS ADMINISTRATION

Chris Clark

57 Corvette Drive • Carson, CO 71121
884.999.9498 • chrisclark@yahoo.com

Education

Benedictine University – Aurora, IL, December 2006
Master's Degree: Public Health
Health Care Administration concentration
GPA: 3.8/4.0

Loyola University – Chicago, IL, May 2004
B.A.: Marketing
Major GPA 3.3/4.0

Experience

Leo Burnett, USA, Account Management Intern, Chicago, IL, Summer 2003
Allstate, Excelon
• Prepared comprehensive competitive analysis tracking Web site content and e-commerce activity for companies including Progressive, Geico, State Farm, and Traveler's
• Tracked activity of insurance companies venturing into the financial services field for Allstate
• Conducted more than 20 in-person one-on-one interviews, coded results, and created research summary for Excelon
• Selected as one of nine interns from a pool of more than 1,000 candidates

Fidelity Investments, Financial Representative Intern, Schaumburg, IL, Summer 2002
• Contacted more than 20 potential clients to determine investing needs
• Routed more than $10MM in incoming funds from 500 clients
• Tracked asset allocation, stock performance, summary of funds, and account status
• Evaluated client portfolios to help balance investment vehicles
• Wrote more than 300 client thank-you notes on behalf of brokers

AmeriCorps NCCC, Charleston, SC, September 2004 – December 2004
• Refurbished used furniture sent to needy communities in Africa
• Helped run Halloween celebration for underprivileged children
• Tutored children at elementary school

Skills/Activities

• Knowledge of Department of Health and Human Services including CMS, CDC, NIOSH, OPHS, HRSA, FDA NIH, SAMHSA, and ATSDR, as well as OSHA, HIPPA, FMLA, MSA, and HIPC
• Fluent in Spanish
• Delta Sigma Pi, vice president of Professional Operations/member, 2001 – 2004
• Habitat for Humanity, volunteer, 2002 – 2004
• American Red Cross, disaster relief specialist, 2004

BEFORE: BUSINESS MANAGEMENT

Jennifer Jeres
82882 Clavin Avenue
Montgomery, AL 52105
(926) 968-9251
jennifer@veres.com

Education: University of Texas El Paso, El Paso, TX
August 2002-Present
Pursuing a Bachelor's degree in Business Administration with a
concentration in Finance and International Business
Expected in May 2006

Arizona State University, Tempe, AZ
August 2001-May 2002

Employment: Cesar-Scott, Inc (International Manufacturers' Representative)
Account Executive
July 2004-Present
Representative of a group of high tech electronics firms whose customers are
in Mexico. Assist customers in processing purchase orders. Complete
weekly action reports to facilitate the movement of material. Identify and
pursue new business opportunities in representation.

University of Texas El Paso Records Office
Student Representative
July 2003- Present
Provide customer service to students by registering them into their classes,
process transcripts, activate returning students and other clerical duties.

Socorro Independent School District
Substitute Teacher
January 2004- May 2004
Substituted in all grade levels ranging from kindergarten through twelfth
grade

Arizona State University Student Financial Aid Office
Peer Representative
August 2001- May 2002
Provided information to students about their financial aid such as Pell Grants
and Stafford Loans. Organized documents to facilitate their control.

continues on next page . . .

Extracurricular
Activities: Delta Sigma Pi
                        Pledge Class President
                        Grand President's Circle
                        Member since 2004
                        Member of this professional fraternity organized to foster the study of
                        business to students in universities.

                        Student Leadership Institute
                        October 2002- May 2003
                        One year program in which students receive specialized training that focuses
                        on leadership qualities to become a peer leader

                        Summer Smart Start Program
                        July 2003- August 2003
                        With the training received at the Student Leadership Institute, a position was
                        attained to serve as a peer leader to incoming freshmen students. Ten students
                        were assigned to each peer leader and served as a mentor to these students
                        transitioning from high school to college.

Honors and
Awards: Monster Diversity Leadership Program 2004
                        Dallas, TX -July 2004
                        Competitive program where only 1,000 out of 10,000 applicants were
                        chosen.
                        Students from different ethnic backgrounds were brought together to enhance
                        their leadership qualities in their particular areas of study.

                        Monster Diversity Leadership Program 2005
                        Ambassador
                        Responsible for recruiting qualified students in the area to become part of the
                        program in 2005

References: Furnished upon request

AFTER: BUSINESS MANAGEMENT

Jennifer Jeres

82882 Clavin Avenue, Montgomery, AL 52105
926.968.9251 • jennifer@veres.com

Education

University of Texas – El Paso, May 2006
Bachelor of Science in Business Administration
Finance and International Business Minor

Experience

Account Executive, Cesar-Scott, Inc., El Paso, TX, July 2004 – Present
International Manufacturers' Representative

- Confirm accuracy of $200,000 monthly in high-tech electronics for delivery to clients in Mexico
- Overhauled commission submission process, dramatically increasing timeliness of payments
- Compile forecasting reports from seven key clients to help insure product inventory is constantly met
- Partner closely with more than 50 client firms to insure steady flow of new business activity
- Conduct business in Spanish with Mexican clients
- Work 18 – 20 hours per week while maintaining full course load

President, Delta Sigma Pi Pledge Class, UTEP, September 2004 – May 2005
Professional Business Fraternity

- Selected to lead a group of 20 fellow students – largest new class in two years
- Organized four fund-raisers generating 35% more income than previous year's class
- Planned and executed Delta Sigma Pi's first volunteer event for battered women's shelter

Ambassador/Participant, Monster Diversity Leadership Program, Dallas, TX, 2004 – 2005

- Selected as one of 1,000 participants out of more than 10,000 applicants for intensive leadership and networking workshop program
- Chosen as Ambassador to help recruit and encourage program participation at UTEP campus
- Conducted 15 class presentations and increased selected applicants from 3 to 20

Student Representative, UTEP Records Office, July 2003 – July 2004

- Registered 100 students per day for classes
- Insured academic eligibility of 50 students per week
- Worked 15 hours per week while maintaining full course load

Peer Leader, UTEP Summer Smart Start Program, Summer 2003

- Selected as one of eight leaders from a pool of 25 to help transition students into collegiate life
- Attended extensive yearlong leadership training program to qualify for program
- Trained in advance leadership techniques, mentoring, and crisis management

Activities/Interests

- Women's Leadership Experience, Participant, 2005 – Present
- Child Development Center, Volunteer, 2005
- Sunshine Center Elderly Home, Volunteer, 2005
- Fluent in Spanish
- Interests include swimming, traveling, Tae Bo, and random facts

BEFORE: PRODUCTION ARTS

Daniel Dean
9927 Dudstone Street, Danes, Illinois 71187
cell: (958) 995-6942 e-mail: dannydisma@aol.com

EDUCATION
University of Wisconsin-Madison
Bachelor of Science in Communication Arts: Radio/Television/Film, August 2006
Graduated with a GPA of 3.4 on a 4.0 scale
Dean's List 6 semesters

ACCOMPLISHMENTS
- Created numerous 3D animations, compositing CGI with live video footage. View my demo reel online here: **www.productions.com**
- Wrote, directed, and edited two independent videos entitled *Dissipation* and *Final Blindness*.
- Wrote, directed, and edited a short video for a major youth group entitled *Leave it to Beber*. This video is shown routinely to chapters worldwide.
- Active member of the UW-Madison Electronic Media Group
- Active member of the UW-Madison Independent Film and Video Collaborative (IFVC)
- Attended Chicago Advertising Federation's 22nd Annual Career Day

SOFTWARE EXPERIENCE

3D animation	Non-linear video editing	Word processing
3D Studio Max	Final Cut Pro	Microsoft Office
Character Studio	Avid XPress DV	Final Draft
Alias/Wavefront Maya	Adobe Premiere	
Realviz Matchmover	Adobe After Effects	

EMPLOYMENT EXPERIENCE
- **AG High Note Productions, Chicago, Illinois**
  Videographer
  Shoot and edit wedding videos
- **Banner Wholesale Grocers, Chicago, Illinois**
  Data Entry/Inventory/Clerk
  Input incoming inventory into database spreadsheets
- **General Cinemas movie theater, Northbrook, Illinois**
  Concession/Box Office Clerk
  Performed variety of duties as assigned
- **Circle M Day Camp, Wheeling, Illinois**
  Arts and Crafts Instructor
  Taught campers, K-5, variety of arts and crafts projects

RELEVANT COURSEWORK

Advanced 3D Computer Animation	Film Styles and Genres
Classical Film Theory	Mass Media and Human Behavior
New Media Studies	Television Criticism
Video Production	Creative Writing: Fiction & Poetry Workshop
Communication Technologies and Society	Advanced Artist's Video

OTHER
- Driver's license with insured vehicle
- Willing to travel and relocate

AFTER: PRODUCTION ARTS

Daniel Dean

9927 Dudstone Street • Danes, IL 71187
958.995.6942 • dannydisma@aol.com

Objective
To obtain a position in the production department at DDB

Education
University of Wisconsin – Madison, August 2006
Bachelor of Science in Communication Arts: Radio/Television/Film
Overall GPA 3.4/4.0
Dean's List six semesters

Experience
Production Assistant, PG High Note Productions, Chicago, IL, September 2006 – Present
- Edited numerous wedding videos using Adobe Premiere Professional
- Developing unique 3D animations and logos for key clients

Writer/Director/Producer, *Leave It to Beber,* 2005
- Created a 15-minute video shown to hundreds of attendees at B'nai B'rith Youth Organization's International Convention in Washington, DC
- Video still used today at conferences and meetings throughout the United States

Project Leader, UW-Madison Electronic Media Group, Spring 2005 – Spring 2006
- Created over 20 3D animations, compositing CGI with live video footage: www.productions.com
- Presented proposal to reproduce cave troll from *Lord of the Rings –The Fellowship of the Ring* using Maya

Writer/Director/Producer, *Dissipation* and *Final Blindness,* 2005 – 2006
- Developed two independent 15 – 20 minute videos for classroom projects

Inventory Clerk, Banner Wholesale Grocers, Chicago, IL, Summer 2004
- Tracked inventory of more than 1000 individual store items
- Created database of items including weight, size, and count

Software
3D Animation: 3D Studio Max, Character Studio, Alias/Wavefront Maya, Realviz Matchmover
Nonlinear Video Editing: Final Cut Pro, Avid XPress DV, Adobe Premiere, Adobe After Effects

Activities/Interests
- Research Assistant, New Media Studies, Fall 2005
  - Wrote proposal on the depiction of race in "Grand Theft Auto" and other video games
- University of Wisconsin-Madison Independent Film & Video Collaborative, Member, 2005 – 2006
- Chicago Advertising Federation Career Day, Attendee, 2005
- Interests include video production, 3D computer animation, screen writing, and advertising

BEFORE: COMMUNICATION ARTS

Lacey Lou
laceylou@bradley.edu

Current Address: Permanent Address:
4000 Joy Lane   2005 Rhames Ln.
Spring Hill, AL 72717   Bay Minnette, IL 71199
419-598-1446   958-999-7977

Objective: To attain a summer internship in the field of creative communications, that broadens my education and work experience.

Education: Bradley University, Peoria, IL
Bachelor of Science – Communications Emphasis on Advertising
Minor: Marketing
Anticipated Graduation: May 2006

Relevant Courses:

- Advertising as a Communication
- Advertising Creative Strategy
- Advertising Design and Production
- Advertising Media Planning
- Personal Selling

Related Experience: East Coast Ad EFX Arlington Heights, IL.
Promoter   Summer 2003
- Executed person to person sales tactics and interpersonal communication to promote local beauty salons and day spas.

LTD. Commodities   Bannockburn, IL.
Internship   Summer 2001
- Revising photography prior to its use in the catalogue
- Assisting in the design set up for photo shots in the in-house studio
- Utilizing skills in photoshop and quirk.

Work Experience: Rosebud Restaurants Inc. Highland Park, IL.
Hostess   Summer 2004

Natalie Alexander Salon and Day Spa Bannockburn, IL.
Receptionist and assistant   Summer '99, '02, '03

Volunteer Experience:

- Books for Guatemala
- Children's Hospital
- Amnesty International
- Alzheimer's Association
- Experience in various soup kitchens and nursing homes

Extracurricular Activities:

- American Advertising Federation
- American Marketing Association

Languages: Fluent Russian and Semi-Fluent Spanish
References and Portfolio:
Available Upon Request

AFTER: COMMUNICATION ARTS

Lacey Lou
laceylou@bradley.edu ♦ 958.999.7977
4000 Joy Lane
Spring Hill, AL 72717

Education
Bradley University – Peoria, IL: May 2006
- Bachelor of Science in Communications
- Advertising Emphasis, Marketing Minor

Experience
Advertising Intern, LTD Commodities, Bannockburn, IL, Summers 2005, 2001
- Served as liaison between production, creative, and Web teams to help produce 200 – 500-page semimonthly business-to-business products catalog
- Styled products for more than 30 individual catalog shoots
- Proofread to insure accuracy of thousands of catalog prices
- Helped design and lay out more than 200 individual catalog pages
- Redesigned comprehensive model comp filing system with more than 600 pictures

Advertising Sales/Graphic Designer, Party Magazine, Chicago, IL, Summer 2005
- Sold 15 individual paid advertisements for start-up monthly magazine highlighting nightlife and after-hours scene throughout Chicago
- Designed five ads appearing in magazine across a variety of categories
- Freelanced doing design and layout of advertising materials and creating and enhancing corporate images
- Worked on layout of entire publication for inaugural two issues
- Increased publication distribution 500% by fourth issue
- Worked part-time while holding separate full-time summer internship

Hostess, Rosebud Restaurant, Highland Park, IL, Summer 2004
- Ranked first out of four hostesses in secret shopper evaluations

Receptionist, Natalie Alexander Salon and Day Spa, Bannockburn, IL, Summers 2003, 2002, 1999
- Scheduled appointments for large-scale operation managing disbursement of clientele across 38 employees
- Collected more than $10,000 weekly in client payments

Activities/Skills/Interests
- American Advertising Federation, Member, 2002 – Present
- American Marketing Association, Member, 2005 – Present
- Amnesty, International, Letter-Writing Volunteer, 2001 – Present
- Alzheimers Association, Volunteer, 2002 – 2004
- Brentwood Nursing Home, Volunteer, 1996 – Present
- Soup Kitchen Volunteer, 2000 – Present
- Fluent in Russian, Proficient in Spanish
- Interests include equestrian activities, snowboarding, tennis, singing, and reading

BEFORE: CONSULTING

Katherine Kiltwitz
P.O. Box 251
Kelpland, FL 44958
(974) 644-4841
kiltwitz@wlu.edu

Education
- Washington and Lee University (W&L)
- B.A. in Economics, June 2006
  - Major Coursework: Economics I & II, Money and Banking, Regulated Industries, Microeconomic Theory, Social Issues in Economics, Integration in European Union, China's Modern Economy, Experimental Economics, Macroeconomic Theory, Industrial Organization, International Trade, Japan's Modern Economy, Central Banking. (GPA 3.1)

Service Experience
- Chairman, W&L Ducks Unlimited Chapter (2004-2006)
  - Planned and advertised the annual DU Banquet, raising over $8500 for the organization
- Chairman, Club 3:30 (2004-2006)
  - Supervised an after school program for Middle School age youth
- W&L Chapter of College Republicans
  - Chief of Staff (2005-2006)
  - Director of Fundraising (2004-2005)
    - Raised over $4000, more than all other Chapters in Virginia combined
- Midwest Regional Treasurer, W&L Mock Convention (2003-2004)
  - Responsible for raising and dispersing funds totaling over $6000 for 11 State Delegations
- Cub Scout Den Leader, Pack 180, Lexington, Virginia (2004-2006)
- Assistant Scout Master, Troop 612, Bartow, Florida (2002-2005)
- Member, Pi Kappa Alpha Social Fraternity (2005-2006)
- Member, Alpha Phi Omega Service Fraternity (2003-2006)

Work Experience
- Insurance Office of America, Inc; Altamonte Springs, Florida (2005)
- Accounting Intern at Carter, Belcourt, & Atkinson, CPAs, PA; Lakeland, Florida (2004)
- Sunbelt Forest Products Corporation; Bartow, Florida (2003)
- PalEx, Inc. (formerly Ridge Pallets, now PalletOne); Bartow, Florida (2002)

High School
- Bartow High School; Bartow, FL
  - International Baccalaureate 3.9 GPA
  - Superintendent Scholar (top 1% in Polk County)
  - Key Club, President (2001-02), Treasurer (2000-01)
  - Varsity Cross Country (1999-02)
  - Varsity Soccer (2000-02)
- Eagle Scout – Bronze and Gold Palms, Senior Patrol Leader

References Available on Request

AFTER: CONSULTING

Kathy Kiltwitz
PO Box 251 • Kelpland, FL 44958
974.644.4841 • kiltwitz@wlu.edu

Education
Washington & Lee University – Lexington, VA, June 2006
Bachelor of Arts in Economics
Overall GPA 3.1/4.0
Dean's List: Winter 2006

Experience
Chairman, Ducks Unlimited Chapter, Washington & Lee, 2004 – 2006
Nonprofit national organization promoting wetlands conservation
- Raised more than $8,500 at annual DU Banquet, highest chapter total in last 10 years and more than any other Virginia college organization
- Planned, organized, and executed all aspects of the banquet attended by 70 students
- Contacted 50 local businesses, securing cash or in-kind donations from more than 20 sponsors
- Overhauled entire organizational structure, creating the first steering committee of eight and establishing succession plan for underclass members

Accounting Intern, Carter, Belcourt & Atkinson, CPAs, Lakeland, FL, Summer 2004
- Researched four industries (coal, oil, construction, and lumber) to provide forecast summaries used for new business pitches
- Wrote company's college recruiting brochure distributed at career fairs statewide
- Confirmed accuracy of general accounts for several client firms

Regional Treasurer, Washington & Lee Mock Convention, 2003 – 2004
90% of student body participates in this 150-year-old tradition to predict the presidential nominee before the primaries
- Selected to oversee 11 state treasurers representing the Midwest
- Raised and dispersed more than $6,000 in funds
- Provided solicitation templates sent to government officials and corporations across the country
- Convention of 1,800 students accurately predicted John Kerry as Democratic nominee in January 2004

Chief of Staff/Director of Fund-raising, College Republicans, Washington & Lee, 2004 – 2004
- Selected to serve on executive board of four representing group of 700 students – largest state chapter
- Instituted the first letter-writing campaign generating $4000 – exceeding all Virginia chapters combined
- Planned and organized 10 campuswide events attended by hundreds of students

Office Assistant, Insurance Office of America, Inc., Altamonte Springs, FL, Summer 2005
- Contacted more than 200 clients to update them on insurance coverage and account status

Activities/Interests
- Chairman, Club 3:30, 2004 – 2006: supervised an after-school program for up to 30 kids
- Member, Alpha Phi Omega Service Fraternity, 2003 – 2006
- Member, Pi Kappa Alpha Social Fraternity, 2005 – 2006
- Cub Scout Den Leader, Pack 180, 2004 – 2006
- Eagle Scout – Bronze and Gold Palms, Senior Patrol Leader
- Interests include reading, soccer, Civil War history, and fishing

BEFORE: CONSULTING

1006 HEMINGBOUGH • ENGINEERY, CA 95419 • (958) 969-5999 • GARRETTALLEN@STANFORD.EDU

GARRETT GALLEN

EDUCATION

Stanford University   Sept. 2004 – current
Economics Major
GPA 3.9/4.0
Coursework includes: Corporate Finance, Introduction to Financial Economics, Risk & Insurance

Northwestern University   Jan. 2004 – July 2004
Full time undergraduate student
GPA 4.0/4.0
Dean's List

WORK EXPERIENCE

Vneshtorg Bank, Russia   July 2004 – Sept 2004
Internship, Strategic Planning Department
Assisted in development of long-term strategic response to entry of foreign banks into Russian market
Researched new business opportunities oriented towards the capture of market share away from Russian
    government's monopoly in retail banking

Center of Financial Technologies   Aug 2002 – Dec 2003
Assistant to VP of Marketing
Responsible for Internet Marketing and Internet PR
Developed and implemented four internet marketing campaigns with a combined budget of over
    $50,000. Projects' estimated ROI was over 120%

ProAvto   Sept 2000 – Dec 2003
Founder and CEO
Created and managed for 2 years internet start-up connecting auto dealers to potential customers
Directly managed staff of 14 people

ADDITIONAL INFORMATION

Leader of Business Plan Competition Team. Assembled the team and currently manage the development
    of a business plan
AKPsi Pre-Business Professional Fraternity, Professional Event Committee
International Educational Opportunities, Head of US Division
Taekwondo Club, Downhill Skiing, PADI Certified Open Water Diver
Bilingual: English, Russian
SAT Math: 800 Verbal: 630

AFTER: CONSULTING

Garrett Gallen

1006 Hemingbough • Engineery, CA 95419
958.969.5999 • garrettallen@stanford.edu

Education

Stanford University – Stanford, CA, June 2006
Bachelor of Science - Economics
Overall GPA: 3.9/4.0
SAT: Math 800, Verbal 630
Will graduate in two and a half years by taking the maximum number of courses allowed each semester

Experience

Strategic Planning Intern, Vneshtorg Bank, Novosibirsk, Russia, Summer 2004
- Improved dramatically bank's bottom line and competitive market situation as part of team that revamped entire banking structure
- Introduced a new revenue center for the bank, creating a way for a city of 1.5MM to pay most bills on-site
- Developed the bill-pay system currently being launched in three other Russian cities, in conjunction with 140 city suppliers
- Played prominent role in bank revenue increase of roughly $25,000 monthly
- Recommended and oversaw outsourcing of Internal Internet banking department, saving money and increasing efficiency

CEO/Founder, ProAvto, Novosibirsk, Russia, September 2000 – December 2003
- Created and managed Russia's first auto-sale Internet company connecting dealers and customers
- Solicited and secured 150 participating car dealers generating more than 1,000 transactions monthly
- Hired and supervised a full-and part-time staff of 14
- Worked full-time while attending high school
- Sold still-existing company to Center of Financial Technologies for substantial profit

Assistant to VP of Marketing, Center of Financial Technologies, Chicago, IL/Novosibirsk, Russia
August 2002 – December 2003
- Managed Internet marketing and public relations for a company of 500 employees
- Launched four separate campaigns including banner ads, pop-ups, and search engine listings with a budget of $50,000
- Generated strong new business results, generating a 120% return on investment

Activities/Interests
- Team Leader, Stanford University Business Plan Competition, 2004 – Present
  - Manage a team of six competing for $25,000 in prize money
  - Professional Event Committee, Alpha Kappa Psi Prebusiness Professional Fraternity, 2005 – Present
- US Division Head, International Educational Opportunities, helping Russian students study abroad, 2004 – Present
- Member, Tae Kwon Do Club, 2005 – Present
- United States Green Card Holder
- Fluent in Russian
- Interests include downhill skiing, scuba diving, woodworking, and Latin American culture

BEFORE: CONSULTING

Amy Allen
aimee@aol.com
1006 OT Boulevard
Cellular 429.732.2171
Twin City, IL, 71192

Education
The University of Iowa, Iowa City, Iowa
Bachelor of Arts, Communication and Psychology, 2006
Study Abroad: Lorenzo de Medici in Florence, Italy, Winter/Spring 2005
Computer Skills: Microsoft Word, Excel, Power Point, Access, and Internet

Employment Experience

2005-Present *Independent consultant* Mary Kay Inc. Iowa City, Iowa
Sell and distribute Mary Kay products to approximately 70 clients. Meet with clients for consultations promoting
health and beauty issues.

2005-2005 *Research Associate/Intern* PMeder&Associates Lake Forest, Illinois
Provided support and research to 3 directors and 2 principals on retained search engagements for both private and public companies. Coordinated research for the entire firm utilizing the Internet, industry directories, direct calls and previous contacts. Managed all office maintenance issues, phones, computer system, and client interviews/travel.

2003-2005 *Sales Associate* D'ancas Home Collection Wilmette, Illinois
Participated in all phases of this retail business including customer sale, service promotion, responsibility for opening and closing of the store, coordination of orders and new advertising promotions.

2002-2002 *Waitress* C.J. Arthur's Wilmette, Illinois
A high volume, demanding atmosphere which required multitask problem solving, efficient teamwork and strong personal relations skills in order to satisfy customer demand.

Activities and Leadership Positions
Delta Delta Delta Chapter Correspondent: Responsible for written communication with the university community locally and nationally, including quarterly articles for the national magazine, the gifts and condolences program, the annual chapter composite and other communication duties.
Delta Delta Delta Public Relations Team: Promoted the ideals of Tri Delta in the community through fundraising events and community support programs.
Delta Delta Delta Officers Council: Elected a member of the leadership team that met weekly to provide direction concerning the business of the chapter including the annual goals, financial governance, membership development, personnel and staffing and public relations.
Reference Chairman: Responsible for compiling and organizing the personal profiles of approximately 400 candidates, leading evaluation discussions and facilitating decision making.
Representative Iowa Hawkeye Hometown Visit: Selected as representative of the Admissions Department to promote the attribute of the university to visiting high school student.

Professional Organizations
Iowa Communications Association

Volunteer Work

2002-Present *Co-Head* Day On The Diamond Iowa City, Iowa
Organized annual community charity softball tournament raising over $2000 for St. Judes's Children Hospital and The University of Iowa Hospital Cancer Center

2002-Present *Volunteer* Run For The Schools Iowa City, Iowa
Assisted in organizing the annual charity run/walk benefiting Iowa City Public schools.

2003 *Meal Coordinator* Ronald McDonald House Iowa City, Iowa
Organized and prepared monthly meals for 30+ people staying at the Ronald McDonald House.

AFTER: CONSULTING

Amy Allen
aimee@aol.com
429.732.2171
1006 OT Boulevard
Twin City, IL 71192

Education
University of Iowa – Iowa City, IA: May 2006
Bachelor of Arts, Communication and Psychology
Major GPA: 3.4/4.0

Lorenzo de Medici Institute of Italian Studies – Florence, Italy: Spring 2005
Studied Italian communication, language, and art history

Experience
Independent Consultant, Mary Kay Inc., Iowa City, IA, September 2005 – Present
- Created a customer base of 70 paying clients via individual solicitations and door-to-door marketing
- Awarded "Star Consultant" for exceeding monthly inventory goals
- Embarking on a "30 faces in 30 days" sales blitz to generate new business

Research Intern, PMeder & Company Executive Recruiters, Lake Forest, IL, Summer 2005
- Conducted extensive Internet research to help McDonald's source a new corporate nutritionist
- Developed comprehensive company staffing lists for targeted employers in the automotive industry
- Created a prospective candidate database tracking all activity on existing searches

Chairman – Reference Committee, Delta Delta Delta Social Fraternity, Fall 2005
- Compiled and organized personal profiles for more than 400 candidates
- Improved quality and number of potential members
- Selected for position by house with 120 members

Lead Organizer, "Day on the Diamond," Iowa City, IA, Spring 2004
- Planned and executed charity softball tournament to support St. Jude Children's Hospital and the University of Iowa Hospital Cancer Center
- Raised more than $2,000, exceeding previous year's total by 20%
- Secured both cash and in-kind donations from local area businesses
- Recruited participants, resulting in more than 400 players

Sales Associate, D'ancas Home Collection, Wilmette, IL, Summers 2003 – 2005

Activities/Interests
- Member, Iowa Communications Association
- Representative, Iowa Hawkeye Hometown Visit – selected to represent the university to visiting students
- Volunteer, "Run for the Schools" – organized annual run supporting Iowa City public schools
- Meal Coordinator, Ronald McDonald House – prepared monthly meals for 30+ people
- Member, Delta Delta Delta Social Fraternity
- Interests include scrapbooks, travel, European politics, and deep-sea photography

BEFORE: ENGINEERING

James J. Janders

Campus Address
#2 Jacklyn Drive
Jeerson, MO 76513
(729) 892-4979

Permanent
2419 Jumping Drive
Jeanville, IL 73357
(618) 664-4460

jjanders@umr.edu

OBJECTIVE   To obtain a full-time position in Aerospace Engineering

EDUCATION   **University of Missouri~Rolla (UMR)**   May 2007
Bachelor of Science in Aerospace Engineering   **GPA 3.1/4.0**

Southern Illinois University Edwardsville   Summer 2004
GPA 3.5/4.0

INVOLVEMENT   **Kappa Alpha Order**
- **President**
- **Crusade Commander**
- **Rush Chairman (2 yrs)**
- **Philanthropy Chairman**
- **Pledge Class President**
- Member of the Brotherhood, Rush, Social, Christmas, and Scholarship Committees
- Participate in intramural sports and various campus Greek events

Greek Judicial Board
- **Cochair**
- A part of first year at UMR

Order of Omega Greek Honor Fraternity
- **Treasurer**

Blue Key National Honor Fraternity
- **Alumni Secretary**

UMR TECHS
- **Cheers Chair**
- In charge of Hot Shots, Safe St. Pat's, and spring break

Rolla Jazz Band
- Play Second (Jazz) Trumpet
- Jazz Band Manager-2 yrs

EXPERIENCE   **Team Seebold Racing** (Bud Light F1 Boat Race Team)   Summer 2003
Fenton, MO
Parts and Rigging Assistant
- Responsible for product quality and parts manufacturing
- Developed skills in fiberglassing and rigging of race boats

Three Pigs B-b-que   Summer of 2002
Lake of the Ozarks, MO
Gas Dock Employee
- Gained experience in customer service and inventory

---

continues on next page . . .

SEARS   Summer of 2004
Columbia, MO
Merchandise Pickup
- Responsible for getting products to the customer
- Gained experience in customer service

COMPUTER   AutoCAD   Word processing programs   FORTRAN
SKILLS   MathCAD   Spreadsheet programs   EES
                Maple   Mathlab

HONORS   Master Manson
                Number I Leadership Institute Graduate (KA)
                Crusade Commander Roundtable Graduate (KA)

AFTER: ENGINEERING

Jim Janders
jjanders@umr.edu
2419 Jumping Drive
Jeanville, IL 73357
618.664.4460

Education
University of Missouri – Rolla (UMR): May 2007
- Bachelor of Science in Aerospace Engineering
- Mechanical Engineering/Aerospace Engineering Departmental Scholarship, awarded for academic excellence
- Overall GPA 3.1/4.0

Southern Illinois University – Edwardsville: Summer 2004
- Overall GPA 3.5/4.0

Experience
President, Kappa Alpha Order, UMR, November 2005 – November 2006
- Won George C. Marshall award in 2006 as one of three most outstanding KA chapters from more than 130 nationally, based on operations, academics, philanthropy, finances, and alumni relations
- Captured top KA award in the nation in 2006 for overall chapter communications efforts
- Reinvented recruiting process, helping increase membership 87% to 56 members
- Increased community service to 200 hours annually per member – highest KA total nationally
- Raised house GPA to 3rd highest of 18 fraternities by introducing scholarship programs
- Removed chapter from social probation by revamping risk management and petitioning university officials
- Selected as KA provincial Most Improved Chapter and Scholarship Award Winner in 2005

Parts and Rigging Assistant, Team Seebold Racing, Fenton, MO, Summer 2003
- Fiberglassed and rigged for Bud Light F1 Boat Race Team
- Built turnover kill switch, automatically shutting down motor in the event of a boat flip
- Refiberglassed a structural crack in boat

Alumni Secretary, Blue Key National Honor Society, UMR, Fall 2005 – Present
- Elected secretary of honorary society, awarded to seniors with strong academics and leadership
- Won "Minor of the Semester" as top member of more than 100
- Write semiannual newsletter distributed to 200,000 alumni nationally

Peer Educator, UMR TECHS, Spring 2004 – Present
- Presented 20 times to a total of 400 students on safe sex, alcohol and drug awareness, and health issues
- Solicited local bars to participate in "Cheers" program serving free soda to designated drivers

Merchandise Pickup, Sears, Columbia, MO, Summer 2004

Activities/Interests
- **Cochair/Founder,** Greek Judicial Board, 2005 – Present
- **Manager/Second Trumpet,** Rolla Jazz Band, 2002 – 2005
- **Recruitment Chair/Philanthropy Chair,** Kappa Alpha Order, 2002 – Present
- **Treasurer,** Order of Omega Greek Honor Fraternity, 2005 – Present
- **Interests** include boats, golfing, hockey, travel, and early American history

BEFORE: ENGINEERING

Will Wilts

42279 Primetime Dr
Sawyer, IL 22320

Mobile: (741) 678-2222
Home: (741)-989-3899

Seeking: Summer internship in technical, engineering based company.

Education: Currently a senior studying General Engineering at Troy University. Degree in General Engineering with a secondary field in Business and Systems Integration expected May 2006. Minor in Spanish.

Fall 2004: Studied abroad in Barcelona, Spain to complete minor in Spanish.

Summer 2003: Studied abroad in Granada, Spain. Learned intermediate Spanish.

Work History: Intern at Crawford, Murphy & Tilly Consulting Engineers, Aurora, IL.
Summer 2004: Learned basic surveying skills with a three man surveying team. Surveyed existing structures for pre-construction plans. Later put in charge of supervising the installation of a new transition main in the City of West Chicago.

Summer 2003: Inspected new construction at Great Rockford Airport. Recorded daily log of men and equipment at all sites, as well as all supplies being used. Compared these to estimates of cost and progress for the project.

Winter 2002-3: Revised plans for new buildings on AutoCAD 2000.

Summer 2002: Inspected and performed tests on infrastructure at construction sites of new neighborhoods and industrial parks in and around Aurora area. Trained new interns when they joined for summer work. Managed new team of interns.

Skills: Proficient in Word, Excel, Power Point, AutoCAD, Matlab, C+ Programming
Communicate and work well with others, quickly learn new information, possess leadership, problem solving, and spatial skills. Speak intermediate/advanced Spanish.

Interests and Achievements:
Eagle Scout: Planned and supervised a 300+ man-hour service project to construct a large observation deck along City of Batavia riverwalk.

PADI Certified SCUBA diver: Advanced and Nitrox certified diver, 60+ dives.

Member of Phi Delta Theta Fraternity: Held position of House Manager for two consecutive semesters.

References:

Jim Kelly
Kelly & Sons
600 Mellissa Way
Birmingham, IL 98943
(782) 454-2234

Courtney Rae
Badger Consulting
(815) 963-9375

AFTER: ENGINEERING

Will Wilts

42279 Primetime Drive • Sawyer, IL 22320
741.678.2222 • willy@troy.edu

Objective

To obtain an engineering internship at General Electric

Education

Troy University – Troy, MI, May 2006
College of Engineering: Bachelor of Science – General Engineering
Business and Systems Integration – Secondary Field: Spanish – Minor

University of Barcelona – Barcelona, Spain, Fall 2004
Studied Spanish literature, culture, and grammar in the native language

Experience

CMT Consulting Engineers, Intern, Aurora, IL, Summers 2002 – 2004
- Surveyed more than 30 construction projects as member of a three-man team
- Examined installation of 7,000 feet of new water main for the city of West Chicago
- Inspected new runway construction at Greater Rockford Airport
- Recorded payload of over 800 tons of construction materials daily
- Monitored costs and progress for $5 million runway budget
- Revised architectural plans for five new structures, including a recreational center and warehouses, using AutoCAD 2000
- Inspected construction of over 25 new subdivisions, each with hundreds of houses
- Performed more than 100 infrastructure tests on sanitary storm pipes, water mains, and water pipes, ultimately failing 50% of contractors
- Trained four new interns

Kam's Sports Bar, Bartender, Chickama, MI, Spring 2002 – Present
- Work more than 20 hours per week while maintaining full course load
- Responsible for reconciling more than $20,000 in cash weekly
- Promoted to head bartender in less than one year

Phi Delta Theta Fraternity, House Manager, Troy University, 2004 – 2005
- Oversaw all maintenance for a housing unit with more than 40 residents
- Launched and executed project to restore and exhibit historical house pictures
- Elected to position for two consecutive terms

Skills/Activities

- Proficient in AutoCAD, Matlab, C+ programming, and Microsoft Office
- Intermediate/Advanced knowledge of Spanish
- St. Jude Children's Hospital "Up 'til Dawn," volunteer, 2003 – 2004
- Intramural soccer and football, 2003 – 2004
- Eagle Scout
- Interests include scuba diving, triathlons, pottery, and the US Civil War

BEFORE: EVENT PLANNER

Diana Dalici

Current Address	Permanent Address
322 Brilliant Lane	4000 Mobile Avenue
Birmingham, AL 61820	Deltaland, CA 60544
(328) 825-1169	(926) 547-2619
diana@shc.edu	

Objective To obtain a job in the field of tourism management with an emphasis on special event planning.

Education

Spring Hill College
Bachelor of Science in Leisure Studies, expected August 2006
Emphasis: Tourism Management
Cumulative Grade Point Average: 3.4/4.0
Edmund James Scholar Honors Program, 2003
College of Applied Life Studies Dean's List 2002
Member of the Phi Eta Sigma Honors Society
Member of the National Society of Collegiate Scholars

Related Coursework:
Independent Study: Created a plan for an African American Arts and Crafts Festival in Mobile, AL
Leisure Service Programming
Cultural Tourism
Leisure and Consumer Cultures
Administration of Leisure Services
Leisure Service Marketing

Activities

Member of Kappa Delta Sorority, 2004-Present
Kappa Delta Bingo Night Fundraiser Chair, March 2006
Attended the Alabama Southland Convention and Visitors Bureau Festivals and Events Workshop, February 2006
Member of the International Festival and Event Association (IFEA) 2005-2006
Attended the IFEA Annual Convention and Expo in Anaheim, California, November 2005
Attended the Intersect Alabama Leadership Conference, 2005
Member of the Epsilon Sigma Alpha, Philanthropy Sorority, 2004-2005
Member of the Spring Hill Masters Swim Team, 2003
Attended the Insight Alabama Leadership Conference, 2003

Volunteer Experiences

Volunteered for the East St. Louis Action Research Project (ESLARP), 2005
Volunteered at the Senior Wellness Convention, 2005
Volunteered at the Alabama Football Fan Convention, 2005
Participated in the Up till Dawn Fundraiser for St. Jude's Children's Hospital, 2005

continues on next page . . .

Employment

Spring Hill College Library
Intern: Book Market @ The Square Coordinator June 2006-August 2006
Coordinated book fair. Created forms, letters, and applications. Formed the
Sponsorship for the event, the budget, the marketing. Worked with authors, book
vendors, sponsors, libraries, and volunteers. Supervised the day of the event.
Created all fundraising activities.

The Champaign Country Club
Waitress, June 2006 – September 2006
Performed customer service, took orders, worked and set up banquets

The Office Bar and Grill, Dauphin Island, AL
Waitress, September 2005- March 2006
 Performed customer service. Take orders, add tickets and serve food.

Camp Akita Summer Camp, Columbus, Ohio
Camp Counselor, Summer 2004-2005
Supervised children 24 hours of the day. Head of the Craft Cabin, prepared and lead
children's programs. Assisted and supervised programs and activities throughout the day.

Spring Hill College Division of Campus Recreation, Mobile, AL
Swim Lesson Instructor, September 2003-November 2003
Prepared and taught swim lessons for children and adults. Taught safety skills.

The Institute for Community, Romeoville, AL
Swim Lesson Instructor, Summer 2003
Created and implemented the swim lesson program. Set up, inspected, and maintained the
pool deck. Supervised the front desk as members entered the facility.

Reference

Francis Meehan, Ph.D.
Director of Library Science
333 Langdon Hall
MC 232
1222 Tiger Lane
Shreveport, AL 61820
(247)-533-4413

Coreil Rider
Academic Advisor
188 Toolen Hall
MC 540
4206 Dorcas Pond
Eleanor, AL 51820
(907)-323-4440

AFTER: EVENT PLANNER

Diana Dalici

322 Brilliant Lane • Birmingham, AL 61820
926.547.2619 • diana@shc.edu

Education

Spring Hill College – Mobile, AL, August 2006

- Bachelor of Science in Leisure Studies: Overall GPA 3.4/4.0
- Edward James Scholar Honors Program, 2003 – awarded to students with a GPA of 3.6 or above
- Phi Eta Sigma Honor Society – membership granted to students with superior academics
- National Society of Collegiate Scholars – admission based on academic excellence

Experience

Event Planning Intern, Book Market @ The Square, Summer 2006

- Planned, organized, and executed first-ever book fair, attended by 1,500 people
- Created sponsorship, bookstore, author, and volunteer solicitations distributed throughout the local area
- Launched major PR program securing placement and personal appearance on WCIA – FOX TV, as well as coverage from four local newspapers
- Handled all preevent logistics including inventory, signage, promotional items, and location
- Developed a multilayered sponsorship proposal used to secure five key sponsors underwriting event
- Organized adult spelling bee and raffle, raising money for the Reading Group – Children's Center
- Managed a group of 30 volunteers and oversaw all day of logistics for event with 42 exhibitors
- Wrote comprehensive manual outlining all aspects of event planning and execution now being used as event becomes an annual tradition

Event Planner – Independent Study Program, Spring Hill College, Mobile, AL, Spring 2006

- Met with city officials, local business, and artists to gauge interest and support for African American Arts and Crafts Festival
- Developed a sponsorship guide recommending potential donors and an approach to solicit funds
- Prepared comprehensive 100-page manual outlining all efforts to execute festival, used by professor in classroom as model for future implementation
- Created a publicity plan listing all local/regional media outlets and tips and techniques for generating PR

Chair, Kappa Delta Bingo Night Fund-Raiser, Spring 2006

- Planned all logistics for the first bingo event, raising more than $1,000 for charity in just three hours
- Canvased the local area to secure more than 20 donated prizes from businesses
- Raised part of $15,000 for Misercordia America, largest fund-raiser out of 62 campus Greek chapters

Server, The Office Bar and Grill, Dauphin Island, AL, September 2005 – March 2006

- Worked 15 – 20 hours per week while maintaining full course load

Waitress, The Champaign Country Club, Montgomery, AL, Summer 2006

- Worked and set up for events including weddings, corporate events, and fund-raisers

Head of Craft Cabin/Counselor, Camp Akita, Columbus, OH, Summers 2005, 2004

Activities/Interests

- Founding Member, Epsilon Sigma Alpha Philanthropy Sorority, 2004 – 2005
- Member/Conference Attendee, International Festival and Event Association (IFEA), 2005 – Present
- Attendee, Alabama Southland Convention and Visitors Bureau Festivals and Events Workshop, 2006
- Participant, Intersect Leadership Conference, 2005
- Interests include swimming, movies, football, running, and reality television

BEFORE: FINANCE

Brenda B. Babbit
594 N. Berry
Chicago, Illinois 60614
(423) 599-1291 bbabbit@aol.com

OBJECTIVE

My interest is to work for a strong organization where I can contribute to a growing corporation.

EDUCATION

THE UNIVERSTY OF ARIZONA, Tucson, Arizona
- Bachelor of Arts in Economics and Italian Studies, August 2006
- General Business Minor
- University of Arizona study abroad program, Florence, Italy, January - May 2004

Relevant Coursework: International Trade Theory, Labor Economics, Economics of Regulation, Experimental Economics, Economics of Futures Markets, Managerial Statistic, Marketing

QUALIFICATIONS

- Highly motivated and coachable
- Excellent written and verbal communication skills
- Ability to apply analytical and critical processes in developing creative solutions

EXPERIENCE

Samlesbury Hall Ltd.   Lake Forest, Illinois   November 2005- Present

- Responsible for inputting and recording daily sales
- Assisted with depositing and balancing daily accounts in Quickbooks
- Updated database of antique descriptions

Economics of the Information Era   Tucson, Arizona   January - May 2006

- Researched current trends in business and Web marketing strategy for team project
- Conducted extensive research on profiled company and competitors
- Collated and analyzed data, reported findings in a comprehensive analysis report.
- Presented results to the class via a PowerPoint presentation.

LANGUAGE AND COMPUTER SKILLS

Computer: Proficient in Quickbooks, Microsoft Word, Excel, PowerPoint, Explorer, and Windows OS
Language: Conversational Italian skills

AFTER: FINANCE

Brenda B. Babbit

594 North Berry • Chicago, IL 60614
423.599.1291 • bbabbit@aol.com

Objective

To obtain a position working in finance in an international organization

Education

University of Arizona – Tucson, August 2005
- Bachelor of Arts in Economics and Italian Studies – Double Major
- General Business Minor

Florence Program/University of Arizona – Florence, Italy, Spring 2004
- Studied Italian Government, Art History, and Language

The Art Institute of Chicago, Summer 2007 – Present
- Continuing education courses in Figure Drawing, Fashion Illustration, and Fashion Design

Experience

Sales Assistant, Samlesbury Hall Ltd., Lake Forest, IL, November 2005 – Present
- Input and record more than $200,000 in monthly transactions
- Reconcile all daily transactions and insured accuracy of deposits
- Wrote product descriptions updating antique merchandise database used by customers and staff

Research Analyst, Economics of the Information Era, Spring 2006
- Researched and presented comprehensive findings on online music category as part of semester-long team project for advanced economics class
- Tracked competitive business strategy, business models, and overall marketplace positioning
- Analyzed cost structure and product offering structure, and researched marginal costs

Server, Happy Dayz Café, Tucson, AZ, 2002 – 2003
- Worked 20 hours per week while maintaining full course load
- Assisted with purchasing, promotion, and construction for new restaurant business

Hostess, Grace, Chicago, IL, Summer 2002

Activities/Interests
- Stocks and Securities Investment Club, member, 2005 – 2006
- Economic Club, member, 2005 – 2006
- Italian Club, member, 2004 – 2006
- Interests include travel, design, cooking, and East Asian studies

BEFORE: GENERAL BUSINESS

24 VENUS AVENUE. • VIOLET, LA 72815

HOME: (419) 773-5711 • CELL: (328) 488-8441 • E-MAIL VINDERBILT@GTE.NET

VANCE VINDERBILT

OBJECTIVE

I am seeking a summer job or internship in the field of Business. With a mixture of creative interests and challenging studies, I would do my best to contribute to the Iona Group Inc. in many different areas of business.

EDUCATION

2004 - 2007   **Louisiana State University – College of Business**   Baton Rouge, LA

- **3.56 / 4.0 GPA**
- Dean's List
- Pursuing B.S. in Business Administration – Marketing
- Expected Graduation May 2007

WORK EXPERIENCE

2006   **The BR Group, Inc.**   Morton, LA

Marketing Intern

- Performed market research, launched a new product, performed market research, coordinated efforts between CEO and web designer, and wrote multiple pages of copy.

2005-2006   **Commerce Bank**   Bloomington, LA

Floating Teller

- Responsible for transactions, cross sales of bank services, assisting customers, and working at multiple locations.

2004   **Heartland Bank and Trust**   Bloomington, LA

Customer Service Representative

- Responsible for cross sales of bank services, assisting customers, telephones, and closing.

2002-2003   **Heartland Bank and Trust**   Bloomington, LA

Teller

- Responsible for transactions, opening, closing, and assisting customers.

EXTRACURRICULAR ACTIVITIES AND AWARDS

- Student Body Treasurer - Louisiana State Student Government 2006-2007
- Treasurer, Captain, & Co-founder - Co-Ed Ultimate Disc Club 2004-2007
- Treasurer for LA Photographers 2005-2006
- Tiger Union Board Photography Competition – 1st Place   2005, 3rd Place 2006
- Bromley Council – Floor Representative and Board Member 2004-2005
- LA Yearbook Staff – Photographer 2006-2007
- Campus Crusade for Christ 2004-2007

AFTER: GENERAL BUSINESS

Vance Vinderbilt
24 Venus Avenue • Violet, LA 72815
328.488.8441 • vinderbilt@gte.net

Objective
To obtain an internship with a consumer packaged-goods company

Education
Louisiana State University – Baton Rouge, May 2007
College of Business: B.S. Business Administration – Marketing
Overall GPA 3.6/4.0
Dean's List Fall 2003 – present

Experience
Marketing Intern, The BR Group, Inc., Morton, LA, Summer 2006
- Served as liaison between CEO and Web designers to create a unique screen saver sold nationwide
- Contacted more than 500 potential clients, securing meetings with the Kansas City Chiefs, Manchester United soccer team in the UK, and the Hard Rock Cafe
- Developed a direct-mail piece sent to major music labels representing talent including N'Sync, Eminem, Creed, and Beyonce
- Wrote copy and launched company's 20-page marketing Web site, www.saveractives.com
- Conducted extensive research project tracking all competitive marketing activity

Student Body Treasurer, Louisiana State University, Fall 2006 – Present
- Appointed to serve undergraduate and graduate population of 38,000 students
- Overhauled all accounting and expense procedures, turning deficit into budget surplus of more than 50%
- Manage and distribute a budget of $100,000

Cofounder/Captain, Louisiana State University Coed Ultimate Disc Club, 2004 – Present
- Grew club mailing list from 15 to more than 700 students
- Petitioned university and secured more than $15,000 in club funds for trips to six different states
- Launched freshmen introductory recruiting meeting/tournament attended by more than 150 students
- Served as Tournament Director for six-team competition in 2005

Teller, Commerce Bank, Bloomington, LA, Summer 2005
- Flawlessly balanced all accounts comprising thousands of transactions across several different months

Activities/Interests
- Documentary Photographer, AIDS/HIV awareness program, Bucharest, Romania
- Photos being used to educate Romanian dentists and attract American dental aid
- Tiger Union Board Photography Competition, 1st Place – 2005, 3rd Place – 2006
- Board Member, Floor Representative, Bromley Council, 2004 – 2005
- Treasurer, Tiger Photographers, 2005 – 2006
- Photographer, LA Yearbook, 2006 – Present
- Interests include traveling, soccer, Italian cooking, and the History Channel

BEFORE: GENERAL BUSINESS

COURTNEY COOLMAN
coutney@wfu.edu

School Address
61582 Rae Parkway
Stargaze, NC 70739
(447) 619-8865

Permanent Address
22 Pistol Pike Avenue
Deltaville, CA 60657
(984) 746-8643

EDUCATION

WAKE FOREST UNIVERSITY, Winston-Salem, North Carolina, May 2006
Bachelor of Science in Business, Minor in Global Trade and Commerce
GPA: Cumulative 3.6   Major 3.9
Dean's List Every Semester

FOREIGN STUDY, London, England, Fall 2004
Enrolled in 3 classes instructed by British professors through Boston University
Traveled independently throughout Europe
Completed a full-time 8 week internship

WORK EXPERIENCE

ADVERTISING INTERN (Summer 2005)
Trone Advertising, High Point, North Carolina
Identified new business opportunities and communicated their potential to senior management
Visited potential clients and secondary sources to gather pitch information
Created full media plan for a large client's upcoming recruitment campaign

PROMOTIONS & MARKETING INTERN (Fall 2004)
20th Century Fox International, London, England
Created a presentation on theatrical/home entertainment synergy for senior management
Coordinated a Fox European promotions conference in London
Assisted in the planning of a Royal Film Premiere

ACCOUNTING INTERN (Summer 2003)
Matheson Tri-Gas, Inc. Parsippany, New Jersey
Developed skills in handling accounts and collecting overdue payments in receivables ranging from $500-10,000
Assisted with preparation of financial documents in Word and Excel
Took part in meetings on the company's long-term financial planning with Japanese parent company

CAMP COUNSELOR (Summers of 2004, 2001, 2000)
Camp Wayfarer, Asheville, North Carolina
Communicated with parents regularly regarding adjustment issues
Chosen to be programming supervisor of all Land Sports and Tennis
Elected to be a member of the Camp Wayfarer Honor Council

ACTIVITIES AND VOLUNTEER EXPERIENCE

WAKE FOREST *LEAD* PROGRAM (Spring 2004)
One of 50 students selected to participate in an 8-week course emphasizing leadership

BIG BROTHERS BIG SISTERS OF AMERICA (Fall 2003-Spring 2005)
Developed strong relationship with my little sister Carrissa, spending time with her at least once a week

CHI OMEGA SORORITY (Winter 2003-Spring 2006)
Publicity Chair, Brian Piccolo Auction Fundraiser
Responsible for public relations with outside community

HOMERUN SERVICE ORGANIZATION (Fall 2003-Spring 2006)
'Meals on wheels'-type organization on the Wake Forest campus
Executive Board Member (Spring 2005-Spring 2006)

AFTER: GENERAL BUSINESS

Courtney Coolman

courtney@wfu.edu ♦ 447.619.8865
61582 Rae Parkway ♦ Stargaze, NC 70739

Education

Wake Forest University – Winston-Salem, NC: May 2006
- Bachelor of Science in Business; Minor in Global Trade and Commerce
- Overall GPA 3.6/4.0, Major GPA 3.9/4.0
- Belk Scholarship – tuition grant awarded to 11 out of 4,500 based on academics and leadership
- Dean's List all semesters

Boston University London Program – London, England: Fall 2004
- Studied economics, international management, and theater taught by British professors

Experience

Advertising Intern, Trone Advertising, High Point, NC, Summer 2005
- Researched more than 30 companies across five categories preparing comprehensive one-page summaries used by senior management to guide new business activity
- Performed extensive research on new business prospects including on-site visits, background documentation, and creative/senior management briefing
- Developed and presented to agency's key client $2MM fully integrated media plan incorporating Internet, newspaper, and direct-to-consumer efforts
- Partnered with youth marketing agency to craft targeted on-campus recruiting strategies used by client

Promotions/Marketing Intern, 20th Century Fox International, London, England, Fall 2004
- Developed a 50-page presentation tracking moviegoer and movie buyer/renter demographics and market trends presented to office senior management
- Planned a Royal Film Premiere for *Master and Commander* attended by Prince Charles
- Coordinated inaugural Fox European promotions conference attended by 20 managers from seven countries

Accounting Intern, Matheson Tri-Gas, Inc., Parsippany, NJ, Summer 2003
- Selected to collect company's most delinquent accounts, ultimately recouping more than $30,000 from 45 different clients
- Attended several meetings on company's long-term financial planning with Japanese parent company

Programming Supervisor, Camp Wayfarer, Ashville, NC, Summers 2004, 2001, 2000
- Promoted from counselor to programming supervisor, responsible for all land sports for 350 campers
- Elected as only one of two staff out of 40 to prestigious Camp Wayfarer Honor Council

Activities/Interests

- **Executive Board Member/General Member**, Homerun Service Organization, 2003 – present
- **Selected Participant**, Wake Forest *Lead* Program, 2004
  - One of 50 students chosen to participate in eight-week course on leadership
- **Publicity Chair,** Brian Piccolo Auction Fund-Raiser, 2005 – present
- **Big Buddy**, St. Alphonsus Elementary School 2005 – present
- **Volunteer**, Big Brothers Big Sisters, 2003 – 2005
- **Member**, Chi Omega Sorority, 2003 – present
- **Interests include** exercise, boxing, sailing, and stargazing

BEFORE: HUMAN RESOURCES

Nathaniel Noswell

Campus:
AGB Nyder 387
317 E. Neabody Dr.
Champaign, IL 72931
(328) 443-2838
E-mail: noswell@uiuc.edu

Permanent:
658 Nordily Drive
Mundelein, IL 71171
(958) 959-9272

OBJECTIVE: I am interested in a human resources position that utilizes my creative and writing abilities. I have taken a variety of courses in HR and would welcome an entry level position to prove my talents and work toward higher levels of responsibility. I have developed organizational and communication skills which give me the potential to achieve success in many positions such as benefits and recruiting.

RELATED EXPERIENCE:
- Interacting with a variety of employees in an office setting as a member of a Human Resources Team.
- Presenting new concepts to upper level management for project approval.
- Research and writing on a variety of topics for the campus newspaper.
- Will graduate in May 2006 from the University of Illinois with a BS in Advertising.
- Cumulative GPA of 3.7 on a 4.0 scale: 3.8 in Advertising studies.

Advertising and other relevant courses taken include:

Creative Strategy and Tactics	Research Methods
Audience Analysis	Persuasion and the Consumer Response
Human Resource Strategy	Social and Cultural Context of Behavior
Development History	Public Relations
Principles of HR	Management and Organizational Behavior

WORK EXPERIENCE:
Human Resources Internships, Summer 2004 and Summer 2005
Fujisawa Healthcare Inc., Deerfield, Illinois

- Helped coordinate and organize the administration of the 2004 Employee Satisfaction Survey and assured the achievement of a 90% response rate.
- Conducted an internal marketing and ad campaign, "YOUR VOICE COUNTS," to motivate employees and let them know that their opinions mattered and were important for company improvement. The campaign included posters, charts, memos, and articles in the company newsletter.
- Benchmarked the company's relocation policy to measure it against Pharmaceutical Industry standards and presented the findings to members of upper management.
- Created a powerpoint recruitment presentation to help sales managers recruit sales representatives. The presentation emphasized the company's strong points, its potential in the future marketplace with new products and also gave a full background of corporate history.

Staff Writer, September 2004 to May 2005
The Daily Illini, **Champaign, Illinois**

-Interviewed, analyzed, and reported on diverse subjects including local politics, student clubs, and other areas of student interest and their daily activities.

ACTIVITIES:
- Staff Writer, *The Daily Illini*, 2002-2003
- Member, American Advertising Federation, University of Illinois Chapter, 2004-present.
- Member, Golden Key International Honour Society, 2004-present.
- Member, Phi Eta Sigma Honor Society, 2003-present.

Nathan Noswell

noswell@uiuc.edu
658 Nordily Drive
Mundelein, IL 71171
958.959.9272

Objective

To obtain a position in the human resources department at Windy City Fieldhouse

Education

University of Illinois – Urbana-Champaign: May 2006
Bachelor of Science in Advertising
Major GPA: 3.8/4.0, Overall GPA: 3.7/4.0
Dean's List all semesters
Golden Key International Honour Society, membership based on superior academics
Phi Eta Sigma Honor Society, awarded to students with GPA of 3.25 or above

Experience

Human Resources Intern, Fujisawa Healthcare, Inc., Deerfield, IL, Summers 2004/2005
- Administered a comprehensive 2004 Employee Satisfaction Survey distributed to all 900 employees, generating an impressive 90% return rate
- Supported survey by developing integrated internal marketing campaign and designing and creating posters, charts, and memos distributed throughout the organization
- Benchmarked company's relocation policy against 25 key competitors, presenting findings to COO, Finance VP, and Human Resources VP
- Created an internal recruitment tool used by sales managers to recruit new sales representatives
- Tracked contracts with more than 100 recruiters, recording contract terms and expiration dates

Research Member, Toyota Matrix, National Student Advertising Competition, Fall 2004
- Generated research results as part of nation's largest student advertising competition
- Handed out quantitative research questionnaires throughout the campus

Staff Writer, *Daily Illini*, Champaign, IL, September 2004 – May 2005
- Selected to write front-page postelection coverage of 2004 US Presidential Election, gauging student reaction
- Wrote more than 10 articles for one of the nation's largest student daily newspapers

Utility Clerk, Dominick's Finer Foods, Mundelein, IL, Summer 2003

Activities/Interests

- American Advertising Federation, Member, 2004 – Present
- Students Against Drunk Driving, Group Leader, 2005 – Present
- Interests include boating, historical novels, painting, and anything related to the Chicago Cubs

BEFORE: INTEGRATED MARKETING

OLIVIA OPPLEHEIM

2582 OVERT ST. • OAKDALE, NJ 19812

PHONE 843-478-1682 • E-MAIL OPPLEHEIM@AOL.COM

OBJECTIVE

A position in the marketing field offering the opportunity to gain experience and utilize my communication, problem solving and leadership skills.

EDUCATION

St. John's University, New York

Bachelor of Science in Marketing, May 2006
- Grade Point Average: 3.9 summa cum laude

PROFESSIONAL EXPERIENCE

Summer 2005   STOS, LLC   Great Neck, NY
Student Intern

- Prepared and executed marketing strategies for Mercedes-Benz Club of America
- Conducted statistical studies for Homeland Security for Sen. Michael A. L. Balboni and Capitol Health Management of New York
- Performed strategic research on various medical societies for positioning of www.stosOFFICE.com medical software
- Interacted with Mercedes-Benz USA, Donna Karan, Giorgio Armani USA, Coach, and Prada for event marketing opportunities on international project in Rome, Italy, with Hon. Rudolph Giuliani
- Assisted in organizing nonprofit organization for event-planning project with the Vatican, James W. Grau, Elizabeth Trump Grau, and Quincy Jones

Summer 2004   Commerce Bank   Cherry Hill, NJ
Student Intern

- Developed comprehensive information databases of seven major NY competitors for use in various marketing promotions
- Compiled Competitor Information Booklets for use by the customer service representatives in the 28 NY area branch locations
- Created databases to file and catalog competitor media sources
- Implemented research on various competitor banks for use in comparison advertisements
- Assisted president of marketing department with database error research

October 2000-Present   Old Navy Clothing Co.   Brick, NJ
Sales Associate

- Extensive experience in customer service and general associate responsibilities
- Created visual merchandising displays according to corporate guidelines
- Selected twice as employee of the month

HONORS

- **Business Honors: Executive-in-Residence Program**
- **Phi Eta Sigma Honor Society**
- **Beta Gamma Sigma Honor Society**
- **Maintained Dean's List standing 2002-2006**
- **Published in the National Dean's List Book 2005**

PROFESSIONAL ACTIVITIES

- **Member of the American Advertising Federation Intercollegiate** Marketing Competition, St. John's University 2005-2006
- **Vice President of the St. John's University Advertising Club 2005-2006**
- Member of the American Marketing Association

REFERENCES   **Furnished upon request.**

AFTER: INTEGRATED MARKETING

OLIVIA OPPLEHEIM

2582 OVERT STREET. • OAKDALE, NJ 19812

PHONE 843-478-1682 • E-MAIL OPPLEHEIM@AOL.COM

OBJECTIVE

To obtain an internship position at OceanGroup.

EDUCATION

St. John's University - New York, NY, May 2006

Bachelor of Science in Marketing, concentration: Integrated Marketing Strategies

- Overall GPA: 3.9, Summa Cum Laude graduate
- Published in the National Dean's List Book 2005, nomination required for consideration
- Peter Tobin College of Business Dean's List, maintained throughout all semesters
- Beta Gamma Sigma Honor Society, membership granted to top 7% of class
- Phi Eta Sigma Honor Society, awarded based on academics

EXPERIENCE

Marketing Intern, STOS, LLC, Great Neck, NY, Summer 2005

- Contacted more than 20 potential sponsors for Mercedes-Benz Club of America
- Tracked census data used in report prepared for Sen. Michael A. L. Balboni of NY
- Solicited sponsorship from companies including Giorgio Armani USA, Coach, and Prada on behalf of Hon. Rudolph Giuliani for charitable event in Rome, Italy

Media Director, VISIT Florida, National Student Advertising Competition, July 2005-June 2006

- Created fully integrated $7MM brand communication plan as part of the nation's largest student advertising competition
- Placed 7th out of 150 school teams at national competition in Dallas, TX
- Selected as one of five presenters for both regional and national competition
- Crafted entire media plan, including analysis of secondary research and development of media selections, including print, television, radio, Internet, and out-of-home media

Executive-in-Residence Program, St. John's University, Jamaica, NY, September 2005-May 2006

- Selected as one of 16 participants out of 350 business students for business honors program
- Worked directly with ADP Inc., Diesel USA, Sugar Foods Corporation, and State Bank of Long Island solving real-life business problems in finance, marketing, and accounting
- Prepared comprehensive reports and presented findings to company's senior executives at headquarters

Marketing Intern, Commerce Bank, Cherry Hill, NJ, Summer 2004

- Prepared extensive analysis and tracked rates and offerings for seven major NY competitors used to help guide marketing promotions
- Compiled bank's first Competitor Information Booklets used by 140 customer service representatives at 28 NY area branch locations
- Tracked advertisements for all major competitors in the NY, NJ, PA area

Sales Associate, Old Navy Clothing Co., Brick, NJ, October 2000-Present

- Asked by management to work full-time during summers and school breaks for last six years
- Twice selected as employee of the month for above-and-beyond performance and adherence to company standards

ACTIVITIES/INTERESTS

- Vice President, St. John's University Advertising Club, 2005-2006
- Member, American Marketing Association, 2004-2006
- Interests includes photography, reading, desserts, and finding the perfect pair of jeans

BEFORE: INTERNATIONAL BUSINESS

Tiffany Tanglow

22 Trixx Boulevard, Rascal, NJ, 51088 Tel:(843) 658-9943 E-mail: tiffanylee@yahoo.com

Objective
To obtain a trainee position in a global consulting firm that delivers culturally connected services and products

Education
Dual Degree Program
M.A. International Relations
Minor: International Business
Seton Hall University
511 Pike Parkway
South Orange, NJ 18219
08/2003-05/2006
*Honors

B.A. International Relations/French M.S.
Saint Joseph's University
6711 Central Court
Philadelphia, PA 19131
08/1999-05/2003

Scholarships, Awards, and Achievements
- Graduate Assistantship: Seton Hall University
  06/2005-06/2006
- Academic Scholarship: Saint Joseph's University
  08/1999-05/2003
- Dean's List: Saint Joseph's University
  05/2001, 05/2002, and 05/2003
- Published work in the John C. Whitehead Diplomacy Journal, Spring 2006 edition

Professional Experience
Graduate Assistant to the Assistant Dean of Students: John C. Whitehead School of Diplomacy and International Relations, Seton Hall University
South Orange, NJ
05/2005-06/2006
- Special student events coordinator for Orientations, Open-Houses, and Student luncheons
- Events representative for high-profile eminent visitors such as Prince Turki Al-Faisal of Saudi Arabia, European Union Ambassador to the United Nations John P. Richardson, and former US Deputy Secretary of State under the Reagan Administration, John C. Whitehead
- Point person for all undergraduate students studying abroad; primary liaison between students and Registrar/Financial Aid Office
- Work with undergraduate recruitment project
- Administrative responsibilities include written correspondence, department inquiries, and data-entry
- Academic advising for undergraduate students

Intern: Office of United Nations Institute for Training and Research
New York, NY
07/2004-11/2004
- Provided logistical support for 6 training seminars designed for country delegates
- Compiled evaluation summaries for seminars
- Maintained contact with high-level diplomats and ambassadors representing various states
- Performed research as requested in the Dag Hammarskjold Library

Senatorial Intern: Office of United States Senator Santorum
Philadelphia, PA
01/2003-05/2003
- Drafted letters for the Senator to constituents and organizations that requested his presence at functions
- Responded to constituent telephone inquiries
- Searched local newspapers for articles containing references to the senator
- Attended formal meetings with community groups, the Director of Economic Development, and the Senator

continues on next page . . .

Educational Seminars
Doing Business in Central and Eastern Europe
06/2005
Graduate practicum in Krakow, Poland and Prague, Czech Republic examining emerging market trends in transitioning Eastern Europe

European Union Study Seminar
06/2004
10 day series of official briefings in Luxembourg, Brussels, and Strasbourg at the European Court of Justice, the Court of Auditors, European Investment Bank, the European Commission, European Council, and US Mission to NATO

French Immersion Program
06/2002
Intensive six-week summer language program at the University of Laval in Quebec City, Canada

Skills and Qualifications
- Proficient in Microsoft Office applications
- Extensive research experience with ABI/ProQuest, Lexis-Nexis, and J-Store
- Intermediate **French** and colloquial **Egyptian Arabic**
- 14 years of international experience gained from living abroad
- Excellent written, oral, and interpersonal skills
- Highly motivated and self-directed

AFTER: INTERNATIONAL BUSINESS

Tiffany Tanglow
22 Trixx Boulevard • Rascal, NJ 51088 • 843.658.9943 • tiffanylee@yahoo.com

Education
Seton Hall University, South Orange, NJ, May 2006
Dual Degree Program: M.A. International Relations, M.S. International Business
Overall GPA 3.7/4.0

Saint Joseph's University, Philadelphia, PA, May 2003
B.A. International Relations: French Minor
Saint Joseph's Academic Scholarship – 25% tuition grant, Dean's List: Spring 2001, 2002, 2003

International Business Seminar, Krakow, Poland/Prague, Czech Republic, Summer 2005
Graduate practicum examining emerging market trends in transitioning Eastern Europe

European Union Study Seminar, Brussels, Strasbourg, Luxembourg, Summer 2004
Attended a series of official briefings at the European Court of Justice, the Court of Auditors, the European
Investment Bank, the European Commission, the European Council, and the US Mission to NATO

University of Laval, Quebec City, Canada, Summer 2002
Intensive French immersion program

Experience
Office of United Nations Institute for Training and Research, Intern, NY, NY, 7/04 – 11/04
- Provided logistical support for country delegate training seminars including International Law of the Sea, the World Bank, and Cyberspace Terrorism
- Compiled evaluation seminar summaries distributed to the Department Chief in Geneva, Switzerland
- Interfaced with high-level diplomats and ambassadors from countries including Nicaragua, France, and Nigeria
- Performed research for Law of the Sea seminar at the Dag Hammarskjöld Library

John C. Whitehead School of Diplomacy and International Relations – Seton Hall University,
Graduate Assistant to the Dean of Students, 5/05 - Present
- Selected to represent the school at receptions for visitors including Prince Turki Al-Faisal of Saudia Arabia, European Union Ambassador to the UN, John P. Richardson, and former US Deputy Secretary of State, John C. Whitehead
- Created school's first alumni file, updating records for more than 1,000 graduates
- Planned, organized, and executed seven "First Friday" events welcoming dozens of freshmen into the Whitehead School
- Awarded Graduate Assistantship Scholarship, earning 100% tuition grant

Office of US Senator Rick Santorum, Intern, Philadelphia, PA, 1/03 – 5/03
- Drafted more than 30 letters on the Senator's behalf to constituents and organizations
- Created database of all constituents applying for Senatorial recommendations for service academies

The Old Mill Inn, Waitress, Spring Lake, NJ, 8/03 – 5/05
Worked 20 – 30 hours/week while attending school to help finance college and postgraduate education

Skills/Qualifications
- 14 years of international experience from living abroad
- Intermediate French and colloquial Egyptian Arabic

BEFORE: LAWYER

2691 Clarkson St. #25   Phone (959) 489-2419
Clonfield, CA 95213   E-mail clasman@yahoo.com

Candace Clasman

Summary of Experience

Education   August 2004 – Present
University of California – Hastings
- J.D. contemplated in 2007

September 1998 – June 2003
University of California – Irvine
- B.S. in Mathematics
- Minor in Psychology
- Dean's List: 1998, 1999, 2000, 2001, 2002, 2003

Experience   December 2005 – January 2006 Juvenile Defenders   Orange, CA
Certified Law Clerk
- Appeared before the court for progress reviews on behalf of criminal defendant clients.

January 2003 – August 2005   Juvenile Defenders   Orange, CA
Investigator
- Interview juveniles at Juvenile Hall and write reports for criminal defense attorneys based on the juveniles' statements.
- Help the attorneys prepare for trial, write orders and motions, conduct research and investigations

August 2004 – December 2004   ACCESS Center   San Francisco, CA
ACCESS Volunteer
- Volunteered to help local members of the community obtain access to legal assistance.
- Aided clients in filing restraining orders and in collecting on judgments won through small claims court.

March 2002 – August 2004   City of Irvine Recreation   Irvine, CA
Softball Umpire
- Responsible for creating a competitive but fair learning environment for girls age 14 and under to play softball
- Responsible for maintaining control of the game and of all its participants
- Responsible for enforcing the rules of ASA girls fastpitch softball

June 2001 – August 2002   IBM   Costa Mesa, CA
Research Consultant
- Responsible for updating and debugging the team's website using HTML
- Researched and collected information regarding the rules and regulations for creating IBM sites
- Participated in minor Java coding

March 2002 – August 2002   University of California   Irvine, CA
Summer Orientation Staff Member
- Volunteered to help incoming freshmen become aquatinted with college life by teaching them about diversity and the college experience through small three day seminars put on in conjunction with other staff members
- Aided parents in dealing with the experience of having a child going away to college by helping to put on seminars discussing these issues

continues on next page . . .

Extracurricular   Volunteered at the ACCESS center, San Francisco   Fall 2004
Alpha Phi Fraternity Member   Initiated   Spring 2001
Phi Beta Kappa National Honor Society   Initiated   Spring 2002
Order of Omega Greek Honor Society   Initiated   Winter 2001
Golden Key National Honor Society   Initiated   Spring 2001
Education Abroad Program, Italy   Fall 2002
Played intramural softball, football, volleyball, and indoor soccer
throughout college

AFTER: LAWYER

Candace Clasman
2691 Clarkson Street #25 • Clonfield, CA 95213
959.489.2419 • clasman@yahoo.com

Education
University of California – Hastings, May 2007
Juris Doctor; GPA 3.5/4.0

University of California – Irvine, June 2003
Bachelor of Science in Mathematics, Psychology Minor
GPA 3.7/4.0, Dean's List six of eight semesters
Phi Beta Kappa National Honor Society, awarded to 5% of the graduating class
Golden Key National Honor Society, membership granted for outstanding academics

Universitá per Stanieri – Siena, Italy, Fall 2002
Studied Italian language and culture in the native tongue

Experience
Juvenile Defenders, Certified Law Clerk, Orange, CA, December 2005 – January 2006
- Appeared before the court representing nine juvenile criminal defendants, handling detentions, pleas, and progress reviews

Juvenile Defenders, Investigator, Orange, CA, Full/Part-Time, January 2003 – August 2005
- Interviewed more than 150 juvenile defendants for a variety of crimes including attempted murder, rape, and arson
- Prepared comprehensive reports summarizing juvenile statements used by criminal defense attorneys to help determine case direction
- Interviewed more than 20 prosecution and defense witnesses
- Prepared attorneys for more than 20 trials through investigating, conducting extensive research, and creating exhibits
- Wrote dozens of orders and motions both independently and with attorneys, including a CI motion and Pitchess motion

ACCESS Center, Legal Volunteer, San Francisco, CA, August 2004 – December 2004
- Helped community members with a variety of legal issues including temporary restraining orders, filing for suits, and money claims
- Volunteered while attending law school full-time

IBM, Research Consultant, Costa Mesa, CA, June 2001 – August 2002

Activities/Interests
- Special Olympics Volunteer, 2005
- Order of Omega Greek Honor Society, 2001 – 2003
- University of California – Irvine, Summer Orientation Staff Member, 2002

BEFORE: MARKETING

29456 Hartman Avenue • Renaissance, GA 71549
PHONE 819-361-5139 • E-MAIL SUSAN@HOTMAIL.COM

Susan Shassetz

Objective

To meet and exceed my portion of duties administered by the corporation that I serve

Education

May 2006   Olivet Nazarene University   Bourbonnais, IL
Bachelor of Science, Marketing

Work experience

May 2003-May 2007   Calvary Day Care   South Holland, IL
Teacher Qualified Assistant
- Maintained positive parental communications, organized and taught lesson plans, and assisted in new employee training

Jul 2006-Nov 2006   Nordstrom, Inc.   Chicago, IL
Sales Associate
- Conducted client follow-up resulting in a 20% sales increase
- Ranked first in department for annual Anniversary Sale
- Received managerial recognition for product placement

Jun 2005-Aug 2005   Bible League   Crete, IL
Research Analyst-Intern
- Conducted research to expand donor base
- Implemented strategic planning for special company events and incorporated direct mail strategies

Aug 2001-Aug 2002   Teen Mania Ministries   Garden Valley, TX
Special Events Recruiter-Intern
- Team deliberated outreach method to target market
- Received recognition for overachieving client confirmations
- Completed one year of leadership/character development program

Summary of qualifications

- Vice President of Communication: American Marketing Association, Student Chapter
- Conducted preliminary market research study for Provena St. Mary Hospital, Kankakee, IL
- Created and completed advertising plan for student project

AFTER: MARKETING

Susan Shassetz
29456 Hartman Avenue • Renaissance, GA 71549
819.361.5139 • susan@hotmail.com

Objective
To obtain a position in the marketing department of Target

Education
Olivet Nazarene University – Bourbonnais, IL, May 2006
Bachelor of Science, Marketing
Overall GPA: 3.2/4.0
Dean's List Fall 2005

Experience
Sales Associate, Nordstrom, Inc., Chicago, IL, July 2006 – November 2006
- Increased individual sales 20% by implementing a personalized sales approach with key clients
- Ranked first out of five departmental sales associates in annual Anniversary Sale
- Recommended and implemented departmental merchandising plan helping drive sales

Cofounder/Vice President, ONU American Marketing Association, Spring 2005
- Launched school's first AMA chapter and grew membership to 20 students
- Crafted club's mission, vision, and recruitment plan, and secured administrative approval
- Spearheaded "real world" educational event featuring mock interviews and networking
- Organized and executed four speaker programs with industry professionals

Market Researcher, Provena St. Mary Hospital, Kankakee, IL, Fall 2005
- Conducted market research at request of client as part of classroom project
- Designed quantitative survey to determine perceptions of alternative medical care including chiropractics and acupuncture
- Conducted 100 phone interviews with respondents
- Presented findings to Provena VP/Marketing

Research Analyst/Intern, Bible League, Crete, IL, Summer 2005
- Researched 200 existing donors to help with effort to increase individual giving
- Sifted through comprehensive donor base to determine viable high-potential givers
- Explored partnership opportunities with more than 10 other not-for-profit organizations

Teacher Qualified Assistant, Calvary Day Care, South Holland, IL, Summers 2003 – 2007
- Worked with children ranging from toddlers to 4-year-olds
- Returned each summer by request of center management

Activities/Interests
- Women's Residential Life, Homecoming Committee Member, 2006
- Habitat for Humanity, Miami Mission Volunteer, 2005
- Save Our Streets, Volunteer, 2004 – 2006
- Interests include travel, exercise, reading, and classic Porsche cars

BEFORE: MARKETING

Zoltan Zanders

zanders@utexas.edu

817 East 35th Street apt.318
Ulysess, Texas 89816
(928) 826-8611

Education

May 2006	**The University of Texas at Austin** Bachelor of Science Major: Advertising Minor: Business Foundations GPA: 3.48

Experience

Spring 2006   **Marketing Intern**, Commemorative Brands, Inc.   Austin, Texas
CBI owns several fine jewelry and paper companies

- Developed brand style guides to define marketing standards among consumer brand products; included standards for copy tone, font usage, color palette, logo unison, and photography
- Conducted in-depth prospecting research to expand $5 million business
- Contacted military personnel to gain approval to use military branch design
- Designed consumer display signs to replace outdated inserts
- Prepared data for budget report

December 2004   **Warehouse Worker**, Integrated Airline Services   DFW, Texas
Summer 2004   *Helped sort a large volume of incoming mail for the USPS in order to meet strict outgoing deadlines*

Summer 2003   **Server**, Chili's Bar and Grill   Grapevine, Texas
Summer 2002   *Handled a high turnover rate in a fast-paced restaurant environment while maintaining quality service and a personal bank*

Activities & Interests

- Terry Foundation Scholar, 2002-2006
- Summer abroad in Barcelona, Spain, 2005
- Helping One Student To Succeed (HOSTS), Fall 2003, 2004
- Phi Kappa Psi Fraternity, 2003-2004

Skills

- Computer: Microsoft Excel, Word, PowerPoint, Adobe Photoshop, Illustrator, Quark
- Languages: Intermediate-level Spanish

AFTER: MARKETING

Zoltan Zanders

817 East 35th Street Apt. 318 • Ulysess, TX 89816
928.826.8611 • zanders@utexas.edu

Objective
To obtain an internship in the marketing department at Pike & Daughters Associates

Education
University of Texas – Austin: May 2006
Bachelor of Science in Advertising
Business Foundations Minor
Overall GPA 3.5/4.0
Terry Foundation Scholar: full four-year tuition scholarship based on academics and leadership
University Honors: Fall 2002, Spring 2004, Fall 2004

University of Pompeu Fabra – Barcelona, Spain: Summer 2005
Studied Spanish grammar, language, and literature in the native language

Experience
Marketing Intern, Commemorative Brands, Inc., Austin, TX, January 2006 – Present
Jewelry and paper company with $300MM in sales and 2,500 employees
* Developed comprehensive logo guide being distributed to internal employees and more than 1000 vendors nationwide
* Surveyed list of 35,000 organizations to select list of top 50 new business prospects
* Contacted representatives of the US Army, Navy, Air Force, Coast Guard, and Marines to secure organizations' approval for ring designs
* Tracked more than 150 monthly marketing expenditures for annual $5MM budget
* Edited and proofread company's www.keepsakebowling.com Web site
* Designed five POP inserts for product displays used at military bases throughout the country

Volunteer, Helping One Student To Succeed, Austin, TX, Fall 2001, 2004
* Worked with students at underprivileged elementary school in Austin
* Tutored 4th-grade boy weekly in vocabulary and reading

Warehouse Worker, Integrated Airline Services, Dallas, TX, Summer 2004
Server, Chili's Bar and Grill, Grapevine, TX, Summers 2002, 2003

Activities/Interests
* University Child Care Center, Volunteer, 2003 – 2005
* Homeless Shelter Food Drive, Volunteer, 2003 – 2004
* Intramural Flag Football, Soccer, 2003 – 2004
* Phi Kappa Psi Fraternity, 2003 – 2004
* Interests include scuba diving, guitar, sports, and Greek history

BEFORE: MEDIA ANALYST

Isabelle Imedine
imedine@vt.edu

Temporary Address:
321 SPH-F
Indonia, VA 35171
(651) 343-7459

Permanent Address:
21399 Indelle Lane
Indello, VA 34227
(915) 661-4357

Objective	Position utilizing leadership and design in Public Relations
Education	**B.A. Communication**, Concentration: Public Relations, Graduation May 2006 **Minor**: Biology Virginia Tech, Blacksburg, VA GPA: 3.01/4.0
Related Experience	**Issue Management,** Virginia Tech, Spring 2006 • Conduct a case study analysis of a public health campaign • Evaluate target audience and the strategies used to influence that audience • Investigate multiple issues surrounding the campaign including, economical, technological, social/cultural, political/legal, and the natural environments **Public Relations Case Studies**, Virginia Tech, Fall 2005 • Design a Public Relations Campaign for a non-profit agency • Campaign includes research, situational analysis, campaign planning, implementation materials, and a client presentation. **Advanced Media Writing**, Virginia Tech, Fall 2004 • Designed a newsletter, website articles, brochure, a radio PSA, and a print advertisement for a local client **Visual Media**, Virginia Tech, Spring 2004 • Designed and developed a personal and professional web page
Leadership	**Alpha Phi Sorority**: Spring 2003-Present • Lady Chaplin: Fall 2004-Present • Director of Campus Activities: Fall 2003-Fall 2004 **Student Alumni Association**: Spring 2004-Present • University Relations chair: Spring 2005-Present • Promote community activities in the area • Lead the association in campus volunteer activities **Ring Dance Decorations Chair**: Fall 2003-Spring 2005 • Coordinated decorating the week of Ring Dance for all committee members • Organized committees, creating themes and ideas for the dance • Handled all orders and budget for the dance **Panhellenic Council**-Assistant to Head Rho Gamma: Fall 2003-Fall 2004 • Co-taught 40 women how to listen and council potential sorority women • Served on executive council which planned and organized recruitment • Coordinated food for 600 women
Employment	**Administrative Assistant,** *Onsite Companies*, Richmond, VA Summer 2005 • Performed general office work and ran background checks • Assisted the sales and recruiting staff in daily activities **Intern**, *Virginia Association of Secondary School Principles*, Richmond, VA June 2004-August 2004 • Prepared, set-up and worked for the Principles Conference in Williamsburg • Instructor for VSCA summer camps, organized and executed lesson plans • Handled multiple phone lines and performed general office work

AFTER: MEDIA ANALYST

Isabelle Imedine
imedine@vt.edu

Campus	Permanent
321 SPH-F	21399 Indelle Lane
Indonia, VA 35171	Indello, VA 34227
651.343.7459	915.661.4357

Education
Virginia Tech University – Blacksburg, VA: May 2006
Bachelor of Arts in Communications
Public Relations Concentration, Biology Minor

Experience
Public Relations Analyst, Advocates for Youth, Virginia Tech, Spring 2006
- Evaluating an existing PR/promotion plan promoting sex education, as part of a school project
- Analyzing a fully integrated program for not-for-profit, including cosponsored foundation efforts, US government relations, in-school awareness campaigns, teacher lesson plans, and Web site
- Tracking all media activity and work closely with client on effort targeting teens, politicians, and teachers

Public Relations Associate, New River Land Trust, Virginia Tech, Fall 2005
- Presented a comprehensive promotion plan to Executive Director as part of student group effort
- Performed extensive research to identify target audience and situational analysis
- Developed $5,000 plan comprising events, premiums, and media relations

Chair – University Relations, Student Alumni Association, Spring 2005 – Present
- Planned, organized, and executed volunteer activities for "Hokie Night," community service event featuring 100 campus athletes and more than 50 student volunteers
- Staffed and supervised "Carnival Day" featuring an audience in excess of 700
- Selected as one of 40 SAA members from an applicant pool of more than 250, and elected as Chair by executive committee and student members

Student Teacher, Virginia Tech Panhellenic Council, Fall 2003 – Fall 2004
- Taught a semester-long, for-credit class educating 40 students on the details of sorority recruitment
- Launched Panhellenic's first orientation magazine distributed to 2,000 freshmen women
- Improved placement results by overhauling campuswide recruitment process

Intern, Virginia Association of Secondary School Principals, Richmond, VA, Summer 2004
- Coordinated logistics and managed registration for two-day conference for 450 high school principals
- Taught leadership skills to 20 students aged 6 – 18 at annual Virginia Student Council summer camp

Chair – Ring Dance Decorations Committee, Virginia Tech, Fall 2003 – Spring 2005
- Interviewed and selected to help plan and execute campus's largest social event spanning two days
- Managed $6,000 and 23 student volunteers in year-round planning
- Worked with university administrators, tradesmen, and fire department to craft a variety of structures including bridges, ships, and a replica of downtown Paris

Activities/Interests
- Director of Campus Activities/Member, Alpha Phi Sorority, 2003 – Present
- Volunteer, The Big Event community service day, 2005 – 2006
- Interests include travel, dancing, sports, and Greek mythology

BEFORE: MUSEUM CURATOR

Emily Eichorn
email: eichorn@wfu.edu

Present Address   Permanent Address
2748 Elder Park Drive   22636 Every Lane
Evangline, NC 38217   Epples, VA 34344

EDUCATION
WAKE FOREST UNIVERSITY, Winston-Salem, North Carolina May 2005
Bachelor of Arts in Art History and Communications
GPA: Cumulative 3.0, Art History 3.3, Communications 3.0, Dean's List 6 semesters

LEADERSHIP ACTIVITES
PUBLICITY CO-CHAIR Chi Omega's Brian Piccolo Silent Auction (Spring – Fall 2004)
Encourage local support and coverage of the second annual auction in October.
Currently have scheduled two television reports, the Winston-Salem Journal, and campus newspaper.
The auction raised over 19,000 dollars last year, the highest amount raised for Piccolo Foundation.

FOUNDER & CHAIR, Student Art Auction (Fall 2004-Spring 2005)
Secured approval and funding from Student Life Office to move forward with this project.
Organizing and contacting former and existing students to contribute works.
All proceeds go towards local Save the Arts Fund for public schools.

KITCHEN MANAGER, VOLUNTEER, Homerun Organization (Fall 2002- Spring 2005)
Coordinated five group meals a week, aiding Ronald McDonald House, the Children's Home, and others.
Created menus to cater to different groups and incorporating our large canned food pantry.
Trained and organized volunteers to prepare and deliver meals.

TEAM MEMBER, Wake Forest Equestrian (Team Fall 2001-Spring 2005)
Senior rider in top division of competitions, jumping and flat.

EXPERIENCE
PRESS INTERN, Bonhams Auctioneers, London. (Fall 2003)
Responsible for reading and cataloging relevant articles into company archives.
Researched auction items and business pursuits for staff members, created images for publications, compiled article books for automobile division, reported selling prices for auctions.
Major project was assisting with Concorde auction November 2003.

INTERN, Exit Art Gallery, New York : Nonprofit Gallery promoting new artists(Summer 2003)
Assistant the General Gallery Manager, gallery moved to Hell's Kitchen in May.
Exposed to all areas of gallery life; development, fundraising, membership, archiving.
Investigated membership trends over ten-year period, created plan to raise recruitment, retain members, the portfolio will be used as prototype to renew a more aggressive membership program.

COMPUTER SKILLS
Microsoft (Word, Powerpoint, Excel), Adobe, Netscape, Pagemaker, Internet Research

FOREIGN STUDY
LONDON, Boston University Programme (Fall 2003)
Courses in Marketing, Public Relations, Art History. Independent travel through Europe and South Africa.

DALAT, VIETNAM, Foreign Service Trip with Wake Forest (December 2004)
Group traveled to build a school through a sister program with the Vietnamese YMCA
Raised over $2,700 to cover personal expense

AFTER: MUSEUM CURATOR

EMILY EICHORN
447.859.8633 ♦ eichorn@wfu.edu
Campus Address: 2748 Elder Park Drive ♦ Evangline, NC 38217
Permanent Address: 22636 Every Lane ♦ Epples, VA 34344

EDUCATION

WAKE FOREST UNIVERSITY, WINSTON-SALEM, NC, May 2005
- Bachelor of Arts in Art History and Communications
- Art History GPA 3.3/4.0, Dean's List six semesters

BOSTON UNIVERSITY PROGRAMME, LONDON, ENGLAND, Fall 2003
- Studied Art History, Marketing, and Public Relations

EXPERIENCE

PRESS INTERN, BONHAMS AUCTIONEERS, LONDON, ENGLAND, Fall 2003
- Managed media desk at Concorde Supersonic Jet auction attended by 35 press organizations including BBC, CNN, and MSNBC
- Researched sell price and descriptions across 50 auction items for English newspapers and magazines
- Revamped automobile division article library, organizing thousands of articles spanning a one-year period
- Perused eight auction-related publications daily and prepared weekly summary report for company president
- Worked full-time and developed comprehensive internship portfolio for class credit

INTERN, EXIT ART GALLERY, NEW YORK, NY, Summer 2003
- Crafted plan adopted by gallery owners to reinvigorate membership at nonprofit gallery promoting new artists
- Prepared comprehensive summary of membership benefits at Guggenheim, Metropolitan Museum, and Museum of Modern Art to help shape recommendations for Exit
- Surveyed 10 years of Exit's membership data to help address changes in member giving habits

FOUNDER/CHAIR, WAKE FOREST SILENT ART AUCTION, Fall 2004 – Present
- Collect more than 70 pieces of artwork across all media to launch school's first student art auction
- Petitioned university and received $2,000 in funding to establish project
- Partner with SECA to generate public interest and attendance at auction
- Built an executive board and assembled a group of 12 underclassmen to make auction an annual event

PUBLICITY COCHAIR, BRIAN PICCOLO SILENT AUCTION, WAKE FOREST UNIVERSITY, Spring 2004 – Fall 2004
- Secured media placements on ABC and NBC affiliates and ESPN radio for Chi Omega Sorority's support of annual university fund-raiser
- Organized auction publicity event attended by Mayor of Winston-Salem and President of Wake Forest
- Raised more than $30,000, 25% higher than any of 12 other campus organizations supporting the charity

KITCHEN MANAGER, HOMERUN ORGANIZATION, WINSTON-SALEM, NC, Fall 2002 – Present
- Coordinate operations preparing five group meals a week for Ronald McDonald House, the Children's Home, and other local charities
- Organized community/campus canned-food drive generating 8,000 cans, exceeding previous total by 100%
- Trained and managed more than 90 volunteers on preparing and delivering food

ACTIVITIES/INTERESTS

- Dalat, Vietnam Foreign Service Trip, 2004
  - o Raised more than $2,700 to cover personal expenses for trip to build a school in Vietnam
- Wake Forest Equestrian Team, Member, 2001 – Present
- *3 to 4 Ounces* Literary Magazine, Board Member, 2003 – Present
- Chi Omega Sorority, Member, 2002 – 2005
- Interests include traveling, running, scuba diving, and fly-fishing

BEFORE: NONPROFIT

Abigail Answell
aanswell@aol.com
Date Available: June 2006

Address:
4539 North Abby Lane
Austin, KY 40001
(347) 840-3439

Education:
- ¤ **University** *of Kentucky*
  Bachelor of Science in Human Development
  Year of Graduation: May 2006
- ¤ **Saint** *Viator High School*
  Year of Graduation: May 2002

Objective:
Full-time employment in the field of human relations.

Volunteer Experience:
» Led and participated with a variety of mission trips across the country and in Mexico
» Served as a leader on ten retreat programs including coordinating an entire retreat through St.
  John's Catholic Chapel and St. Edna Parish through high school and college
» Served at soup kitchens and HIV Coalition on a dependable bi-weekly basis

Recognition
» Pioneer Press Volunteer of the Year 2002
» Catholic Youth Organization Leadership Award 2000, 2001, and 2002
» Frontier Days Leadership in Volunteer Scholarship

Employment Experience:
- ¤ **Summer Intern • Catholic HEART Workcamp (Orlando, FL) • Summer 2005**
  » Selected from a competitive field of applicants representing the entire country
  » Helped lead interactive activities and nightly presentations
  » Worked as a team to develop a mission experience for 400 high school students per week
  » Acted as a liaison between students, youth ministers, and adult leaders
- ¤ **Secretary • St. Edna Parish (Paducah, KY) • August, 2002 – August, 2005**
  » Used Microsoft Office to facilitate bulletin layout and organization
  » Worked as a connection between office employees performing general duties
  » Assisted with parish appeals and social assistance
- ¤ **Counselor • Buffalo Grove Park District (Buffalo Grove, KY) • Summers 2000-2005**
  » Worked to create a safe environment
  » Worked as a link between parents, children, and staff
  » Established a creative environment for individuals to grow and learn

AFTER: NONPROFIT

Abigail Answell

4539 North Abby Lane • Austin, KY 40001
347.840.3439 • aanswell@aol.com

Objective
To obtain a position working for a charitable organization

Education
University of Kentucky – Lexington: May 2006
Bachelor of Science in Human Development
Overall GPA: 3.7/4.0
Frontier Days Leadership in Volunteer Scholarship – tuition grant based on outstanding commitment, volunteer work, and leadership

Experience
Intern, Catholic HEART Work Camp, Orlando, FL, Summer 2005
- Traveled 3,000 miles to eight different US cities facilitating weeklong mission trips for thousands of high school students
- Delivered weekly motivational/educational speeches, and emceed overall program presented to more than 3,000 teenagers
  o Speech selected to be taped and shown to archbishop to help secure program funding
- Coordinated $8,000 worth of merchandise used to generate funds for charitable causes
- Acted as a liaison between students, hundreds of youth ministers, and dozens of adult leaders
- Selected as one of just 70 interns from a competitive national pool of candidates

Retreat Coordinator, St. John's Catholic Chapel, Lexington, KY, Fall 2002 – Present
- Selected as student leader for 10 separate retreats during college
- Delivered presentations, coordinated music, and helped facilitate logistics for dozens of students
- Planned, organized, and executed retreat event for 40 participants and 200 community members
- Facilitated logistics including meetings, transportation, and overall program scheduling

Counselor, Buffalo Grove Park District, Buffalo Grove, KY, Summers 2000 – 2005
Secretary, St. Edna Parish, Paducah, KY, August 2002 – August 2005
Student Leader/Participant, Mission Trips, US and Mexico, 2000 – Present

Activities/Interests
- Street Team Member, BMX music groups, 2003 – Present
- Soup Kitchen Volunteer, St. Jude's Catholic Worker House, 2002 – Present
- HIV Coalition Volunteer, 2002
- Intramural Football/Basketball, 2002 – Present
- Interests include reading, sports, travel, music, and Italian cooking

BEFORE: PUBLIC RELATIONS

Muriel Mooney

Muriel@yahoo.com

Current Address:		**Permanent Address:**
552 N. Woodland View		3516 Greenwell Springs Road
Landry, IN 58519		Central, IL 71136
(923) 446-5517/Cell: (958) 319-8784		(958) 383-3696

OBJECTIVE

To obtain a position in the field of advertising and/or public relations that will utilize my previous marketing experience and strong communication skills.

EDUCATION

Indiana University	Bloomington, IN	May 2006 Bachelor
of Arts, Journalism		G.P.A. 3.3/4.0
International Education of Students	London, England	January-May 2005

Edward L. Hutton International Experience Grant, granted to students with a GPA of 3.0 or above.

WORK EXPERIENCE

Clear Channel	Chicago, IL	Summer 2005
Intern		

- Departmental Liaison for all promotional events for 103.5 KISS FM.
- Corresponded with vendors regarding upcoming concerts and station events.
- Operated various on-premise appearances and station events.
- Managed and organized prize fulfillment and listeners inquiries.
- Assisted in strengthening relationship with clients by organizing client party.

DRAFT	Chicago, IL	Summer 2004 *Intern*

- Assisted Account Services team on Ross Products account.
- Reinvented the Welcome Addition Club through Direct Marketing for Similac Infant Formulas.
- Led process to develop and evaluate content management system, Vioma, with outside vendors.
- Organized and managed change forms for the creative team to further the process of updating Similac mailings.
- Designed PowerPoint presentation for client to display visuals for the Similac 2004 Photo Shoot.

Valley Lo Sports Club	Glenview, IL	2000-2004
Lifeguard		

- Learned to quickly assess potentially dangerous situations and determine appropriate action.
- Ensured safety of swimmers and boaters.

ACTIVITIES AND HONOR

- Kappa Alpha Theta Sorority member at Indiana University 2003-Present
- Senior Leader for Kappa Alpha Theta Recruitment Committee 2005-2006
- International Association of Business Communicators: IABC 2004-2006
- Indiana University Dance Marathon Promotions Chair for the Ryan White Infectious Disease Center at Riley Hospital for Children 2004

AFTER: PUBLIC RELATIONS

Muriel Mooney
Muriel@yahoo.com ◆958.383.3696

Current Address:	**Permanent Address:**
552 N. Woodland View	3516 Greenwell Springs Road
Landry, IN 58519	Central, IL 71136

OBJECTIVE
To obtain a position in the public relations department at Draft

EDUCATION
Indiana University – Bloomington, May 2006
Bachelor of Arts-Journalism, Concentration-Communications
GPA: 3.3/4.0
International Education of Students, London, England, Spring 2005
Edward L. Hutton International Experience Grant, awarded to students with a GPA of 3.0 or above
Studied British communications, architecture, and culture

EXPERIENCE
Promotions Intern, Clear Channel – *103.5 KISS FM*, Chicago, IL, Summer 2005
- Worked on 30 on-site events throughout the regional area collecting listener names, handing out promotional materials, and setting up remote broadcasts
- Organized thousands of dollars in station giveaways including vacations, cars, and concert tickets
- Performed dozens of site checks and coordinated more than 20 events for clients including McDonald's, Great America, and Jewel-Osco
- Executed and assisted with station presentation/social event at the W Hotel for 40 key clients including Meijer, Dr. Pepper/7-Up, and Dairy Queen

Account Management Intern, Draft – *Similac Infant Formulas*, Chicago, IL, Summer 2004
- Overhauled Similac Welcome Addition Club featuring 12 separate mailings distributed to more than 1.8 million women
- Managed change form process for several direct mailings including copy editing, layout recommendations, and content updates
- Worked with outside vendor to evaluate proprietary agency/client extranet site managing creative production
- Developed a client presentation analyzing preproduction shot recommendations for photo shoot

Promotions Chair, Indiana University Dance Marathon, 2004
- Selected as 1 of 12 from a pool of 200 applicants to handle all promotional activity for school's largest student fund-raiser and 3rd largest student-run organization in the country
- Contacted more than 15 area businesses to help generate publicity and support for the event
- Raised more than $2,000 to support event, which generated over $400,000 in donations
- Visited campus dorms to create interest and help attract more than 500 total participants

Lifeguard, Valley Lo Sports Club, Glenview, IL, Summer 2000-2004

ACTIVITIES AND INTERESTS
- International Association of Business Communicators, member, 2004-present
- Kappa Alpha Theta Cochairman of Recruitment Committee/member, 2003-present
- Hoosier Hills Bike Tour, Volunteer, 2003-present
- Intramural Volleyball, 2003-present
- Interests include sports, traveling, and attending various concerts

BEFORE: SALES

Flora Flurston
fflurston@hotmail.com

(728) 379-9981
545 Ferry 5th Street
Boston, MA 13238

SPECIAL SKILLS:	French language, Advanced in Microsoft Word, Access, Excel, PowerPoint. Internet proficient.
EDUCATION: (2003-2007)	Lehigh University Bethlehem, PA B.S. in Marketing, Minor in French - May 2005 Major GPA: 3.77
January-June 04	University of Minnesota Study Abroad Program, Montpellier, France. Studied Marketing and French Business Affairs while completing a minor in the French Language
RELATED COURSES:	Money and Banking, Business Information Systems, Marketing Communications, Business-to-Business Marketing, Marketing Research

PROFESSIONAL WORK HISTORY:

Escada, Boston, MA   December 05-June 06
-A luxury brand clothing boutique – **Operations Administrator**
- Served as the senior support to the store manager
- Processed all outgoing transfers and damages; received and verified all incoming merchandise
- Packaged and shipped all outgoing merchandise
- Hands-on support executing seasonal inventory
- Stockroom and sales floor organization regularly
- Corporate weekly mail pack including receipt log, sales tax log, and sales audit
- Accounts payable functions including submission of invoices
- Placed monthly supply orders as well as reordered office supplies as needed
- Timekeeping and payroll
- Sales floor assistance selling store merchandise; catered to customer service needs and requests

Marketing Practicum (MKT 360)   August 04-December 04
-A college-level course elective - **Team Member**
- Developed a complete marketing plan for a real client looking to introduce an innovative idea for an electronic product to market
- Conducted field research, team meetings, interviews
- Presented plan in the form of an extensive PowerPoint presentation

Knight Securities, Jersey City, NJ.   June 02-August 02
-Brokerage firm that provides trade execution services in cash equities and equity options as well as asset management services. - **Intern**
- Provided administrative support to the sales manager as well as the traders.
- Duties included updating equipment records, entering data into spreadsheets, contacting suppliers.
- Extensive filing and message distribution
- Received training in Bloomberg computer program and execution of trade operations

Murphy Durieu, Hauppauge, NY   June 01- August 01
-Brokerage firm that provides bond and equity execution services primarily for institutions in addition to retail. - **Intern**
- Provided administrative office support to traders and secretaries
- Duties included answering and connecting phone calls, organizing files, updating files
- Aided traders setting up new accounts by completing and organizing related paperwork

TRAVEL: **ACTIVITIES/**	Recent travel experience includes Spain, Italy, Greece, France Swiss Challenge Snowboard Camp in Zermatt, Switzerland
AWARDS:	Gamma Phi Beta Sorority Member (off-campus relations manager), Community Service at Blough Nursing Home.

AFTER: SALES

Flora Flurston

545 Ferry 5th Street • Boston, MA 13238
728.379.9981 • fflurston@hotmail.com

Objective
To obtain a position in the sales department at Pepsi

Education
Lehigh University – Bethlehem, PA, May 2005
B.S.: Marketing, Minor: French
Major GPA: 3.8/4.0
Dean's List, Fall 2004, Spring 2005

University of Minnesota Study Abroad Program – Montpellier, France, Spring 2004
Studied Marketing and French Business Affairs in the native language

Experience
Escada, Operations Manager, Boston, MA, December 2005 – June 2006
- Processed more than $35,000 weekly in merchandise transfers at luxury brand clothing boutique
- Audited in excess of 100 sales tax receipts monthly to verify proper payments across multiple states
- Tracked all store cash, check, and gift certificate receipts
- Coordinated timekeeping for seven employees, triggering payroll from national office
- Confirmed monthly shipments of more than $100,000 in store merchandise
- Monitored and paid all store bills including supplies, utilities, and miscellaneous expenses

Bonner Business, Team Member, Lehigh University, Fall 2004
- Developed an integrated marketing plan for a building product as part of class project
- Prepared pricing analysis, conducted qualitative phone interviews, and created marketing strategy
- Presented final plan to client

Knight Securities, Intern, Jersey City, NY, Summer 2002
- Prepared comprehensive trader's journal tracking employee activity
- Updated approved users for computer system for 150 traders
- Trained in execution of trade operations and in Bloomberg computer system

Activities/Interests
- Lehigh University Good Scholar Program, Volunteer, 2001 – 2005
- City of Bethlehem, City Cleaning Volunteer, 2004
- Gamma Phi Beta Sorority, Member, 2001 – 2005
- Completed Athens Marathon, 2005
- Interests include travel, cooking, snowboarding, and sports

BEFORE: RESEARCH SCIENTIST

Ashley Arcineaux
123 St. Ignatious Street Apt. ABC, Teacherly, CA 53082
Phone (919) 594-9554 Fax (919) 493-9444 E-mail ashley@robicheaux.com

<u>Objective</u>

> To attain a position in an innovative, gerontology-oriented organization where my experience
> and enthusiasm will have application, and new knowledge and skills can be acquired

<u>Qualifications/Skills</u>

- Certified Social Worker in the state of Wisconsin
- proficiency in Spanish language
- strong oral and written communication ability
- computer and Internet literate
- member American Society on Aging

<u>Education</u>

University of La Verne, La Verne, CA (anticipated graduation: 8/2006)
Master of Science,   Gerontology Administration
University of Iowa, Iowa City, Iowa (1995-1999)
B.A., Social Work, 3.5 GPA
Minor, Spanish
Universidad Nacional, Heredia, Costa Rica (fall semester 1999)
4.0 GPA

<u>Employment Experience</u>

Odyssey Health Care, Inc., West Allis, WI
  Medical Social Worker (5/03-8/05)
   Provision of continued overall assessment of psychosocial well-being and monitoring of comfort level to
   persons requiring end-of-life care in a hospice setting
   Provision of support and empathic awareness to patients and their family members
   Consultation with medical professionals to provide quality continuum of patient care
Virginia Highlands Health Center, Germantown, WI
  Director of Social Services (2/03-5/03)
   Assumption of administrative authority and accountability for the provision of medically
   related social services to residents in a long-term, Alzheimer's, and subacute care facility
   Supervision of facility social workers and guidance of facility staff in matters of residency advocacy,
   protection, and promotion of residents' rights
   Administrative collaboration in allocation of resources in efficient and economic manner
Mercy Residential Center, Milwaukee, WI
  Director of Social Services (11/01-2/03)
   Provision of direct and supportive services to residents, family members, and members of the community to
   promote maximum benefit from the health-care services provided
Therapeutic Advocacy and Support Centers (TASC), Boston, MA
  Manager (6/01-7/01)
   Management and supervision of support staff and clientele during off-site tours
Leon Resource Center, Tallahassee, FL
  Supported Living Counselor (6/00-12/00)
   Provision of daily living services to persons with developmental disabilities
   Management of financial accounts and active as a liaison between client and
   governmental entities
University of Iowa Chemical Dependency Center, Iowa
Addictions Counselor Intern (5/99-8/99)

AFTER: RESEARCH SCIENTIST

Ashley Arcineaux

123 St. Ignatious Street. Apt. ABC • Teacherly, CA 53082
919.594.9554 • Ashley@robicheaux.com

Education
University of La Verne – La Verne, CA: August 2006
Master of Science in Gerontology, Administration Minor, Overall GPA 3.9/4.0
Completing full-time two-year program in one year
Thesis: Assistive Devices: Medical Necessities or Lifestyle Accessories?

University of Iowa – Iowa City: December 1999
Bachelor of Arts in Social Work, Spanish Minor, Major GPA 3.5/4.0

Universidad Nacional – Heredia, Costa Rica: Fall 1999
Studied grammar, language, history, and drama in Spanish

Experience
Gerontology Intern, Silverado Senior Living, Azusa, CA, 4/06 – Present
- Visited six dementia-care facilities throughout southern California to gauge care programs
- Prepared extensive competitive analysis, tracking staffing, living costs, facilities, and level of care, used by marketing department to drive corporate strategy

Medical Social Worker, Odyssey Health Care, Inc., West Allis, WI, 5/03 – 8/05
- Helped patients suffering from cancer, dementia, Parkinson's, Alzheimer's, emphysema, and more
- Worked with interdisciplinary team of physicians, nurses, clergy, and home health aides
- Assessed psychological well-being and monitored comfort level of more than 500 patients and families in a hospice setting
- Counseled families on diverse issues including power of attorney, Medicare, and funeral planning

Director of Social Services, Virginia Highlands Health Center, Pixie, WI, 2/03 – 5/03
- Managed administrative issues including patient discharge planning, family counseling, and social worker oversight for 100-bed facility
- Instructed facility staff on topics including residency advocacy and protection of patient rights

Director of Social Services, Mercy Residential Center, Milwaukee, WI, 11/01 – 2/03
- Conducted more than 10 in-service trainings for a staff of 75 long-term care providers
- Advocated to community and families for patient rights, privacy issues, and informed consent
- Worked extensively with Department on Aging, providing more than 200 patients with a host of available resources

Supported Living Counselor, Leon Resource Center, Tallahassee, FL, 6/00 – 12/00

Activities/Interests
- American Society on Aging, Member, 2005 – Present
- Wisconsin Certified Social Worker
- Interests include design, horseback riding, travel, running, and antique lamps

BEFORE: SOCIAL WORKER

Daniel Duncatz

9311 Denverria Way #222
Dunlap, CA 94422
772-916-7472
danieldun@hotmail.com

Areas of Specialty	
• Adolescent • Adult • Geriatric • Mental Disorders	• Substance Abuse • PTSD • Work Stress • Relational Problems

Education		
	Master of Social Work – IN PROGRESS *California State University, Bakersfield* **Bachelor of Science in Liberal Studies** *National University*	*Sept 2005 – June 2007* *Sept 2003- April 2005*

Experience   **SOCIAL SERVICES**, Bakersfield, California

June 2005 - Present

Kaiser Permanente - Student Therapist

- Conduct biopsychosocial assessment and diagnosis.
- Formulate treatment plans.
- Provide therapeutic services using individual, couples, family, and group treatment.

Good Samaritan Hospital – Psychiatric/Medical Social Worker

- Conducted biopsychosocial evaluations.
- Provided therapeutic intervention services to patients.
- Coordinated Inter-Disciplinary Treatment meetings with staff and patient.
- Provided linkage between patient and community resources.

Bakersfield Memorial Hospital - Student Medical Social Worker

- Conducted biopsychosocial evaluations.
- Counseled individuals, families, and groups.
- Provided crisis intervention.
- Provided linkage between patient and community resources.

Kern County Mental Health – Recovery Specialist Aide
- Formulated treatment plans that addressed client's needs.
- Arranged and coordinated the delivery of client services.
- Served as the central point of responsibility and communication for client.
- Advocated for clients within the complex system of services

Experience   **LAW ENFORCEMENT**, Kern County, California

August 1987 – April 2004

Bakersfield Police Department – Retired Police Officer

Taft Police Department

Kern County Sheriff's Department

Ridgecrest Police Department

AFTER: SOCIAL WORKER

Daniel Duncatz

9311 Denverria Way #222 • Dunlap, CA, 94422
772.916.7472 • danieldun@hotmail.com

Education
California State University – Bakersfield, June 2007
- **Master of Social Work**
- Health and Mental Health Concentration
- Overall GPA: 3.8/4.0

National University – Bakersfield, CA, April 2005
- **Bachelor of Science in Liberal Studies**
- Overall GPA: 3.9/4.0

Experience
Student Therapist, <u>Kaiser Permanente</u>, Bakersfield, CA, September 2006 – Present
- Manage an ongoing caseload of 20 patients suffering from anxiety, depression, mental illness, and more
- Prepare a wide variety of treatment plans for all new patients using strengths perspective, social systems theory, and cognitive behavioral therapy
- Conducted more than 50 independent biopsychosocial assessments and diagnoses for patients ranging from adolescents to geriatrics
- Selected as organization's first student therapist social worker

Psychiatric/Medical Social Worker, <u>Good Samaritan Hospital</u>, Bakersfield, CA
January 2006 – September 2006
- Conducted 250 independent biopsychosocial evaluations of the chronically mentally ill
- Provided independent cognitive therapeutic intervention services to hundreds of patients
- Worked closely with physicians, nurses, and patients facilitating interdisciplinary treatment meetings typically handled by MSW graduates
- Managed patient discharge program, serving as liaison between patients and government/community resources
- Worked 40 hours per week while attending school full-time

Student Medical Social Worker, <u>Bakersfield Memorial Hospital</u>, Bakersfield, CA
September 2005 – January 2006
- Conducted 25 biopsychosocial assessments on patients primarily suffering from illness-related mental issues
- Counseled individuals, families, and groups in a variety of environments

Recovery Specialist Aide, <u>Kern County Mental Health</u>, Bakersfield, CA, Summer 2005
- Managed a caseload of 10, serving as case manager
- Developed comprehensive treatment plans covering issues from diagnosis to social service resource coordination

Police Officer, Kern County, CA, August 1987 – April 2004

Sample Cover Letters

Category 1:
Strong Passion for Job Responsibilities

Return Address

Recipient Address

Dear Ms. Smith:

I think I might be obsessed with design.

Not obsessed in a bad way, but obsessed as in not being able to get enough of it.

For me, it's about developing concepts. It's about coming up with new ideas and new ways to look at a problem. It's about laying something out and realizing it's the perfect blend of aesthetics.

I've been lucky. I've had some incredible design experience in the last few years. I've worked as a full-time designer for *Fort Worth Weekly Magazine*, I've developed entire magazine comps for a new upscale publication, and I've even created Web sites, DVD materials, and more. All the details are in my portfolio and resume.

I'm excited to parlay my experience into a full-time position at *Vogue* magazine. I'll be moving to New York on September 3rd and would love the opportunity to talk more about possibilities at the magazine.

I'll plan to contact you in about a week. If you'd like to reach me in the meantime, my mobile number is below.

Regards,

Sandy Samford
343.676.2367

Return Address

Recipient Address

Dear Mr. Smith:

Why would an established stockbroker give up a lucrative career and go back to school to become an editor?

It's easy. Passion.

Finding one's true calling is much more valuable than making a lot of money in an unsatisfying career. I knew from the moment I cut my first piece of film that I made the right decision. Our first school project was to cut stock with a razor. I thought they were nuts to make us do it. But once I got started, they had to drag me out of the classroom! I was hooked, and it's only gotten better.

I know that I'm a nontraditional candidate. I know I'm going to have to work hard and prove myself over and over again. At the same time, I am supremely confident that I have the skills and the desire to be successful.

When I'm in the editing room, I'm happy, passionate, and dedicated. Nothing else matters.

I look forward to speaking with you in more detail about opportunities at Strategic Solutions. I'll plan to follow up with you in a week.

Regards,

Dominick Dante
452.933.0236

Return Address

Recipient Address

Dear Ms. Smith:

I feel like the office manager job is tailor made for me.

The combination of organizational/executional skills with an eye for the creative is what truly intrigues me.

Quite simply, I love details. Right now, I work as the office manager for one of the city's most respected architects. I handle everything that makes the office tick. And I do mean everything. From organizing thousands of architects' files to handling the entire payroll and even managing office supplies, I do it all.

For me, there's very little more satisfying than making sure a project runs smoothly, efficiently, and on budget.

On the other hand, I feel extremely comfortable in a creative environment.

I studied photography for four years at college. And while my days behind the camera are over, I still love a creative atmosphere. I have a great sense of layout and design, and I am quite familiar with all aspects of urban planning.

Peabody is a wonderful company. I work with all the major Dallas agencies, and I only hear good things about your company. I'd love the chance to parlay my skills into a long career at Peabody.

I'll plan on touching base shortly.

Regards,

Lauren Lindberg
349.343.0913

Return Address

Recipient Address

Dear Mr. Smith:

"We're looking for people with boundless drive and determination, aggressive entrepreneurial go-getters who welcome the challenge of unlimited possibilities and the chance to make the most of their abilities."

I can't imagine a better way to describe me and what I crave in a career. I also can't imagine a better position for me than as a Financial Consultant at Smith Barney.

My sales experience at Escada, my tenacity, and my financial background at Knight Securities help make me an ideal candidate for this position. I aspire to be an entrepreneur, and I know with the right training and tools I can be extremely successful.

I look forward to speaking in more detail with you about the Financial Consultant position and will plan to follow up in a week's time.

Regards,

Megan Mauve
617.254.0804

Return Address

Recipient Address

Dear Ms. Smith:

I consider myself to be quite the juggler.

Not in the classic "clown at the circus" sense, but as it relates to thriving in an environment when I'm juggling task after task.

Since October I've worked as a coordinator at a salon with more than 100 employees and thousands of customers a week. Customer service, attention to detail, multitasking, and error-free work are an absolute necessity. I'm sure you can imagine the demands of salon clientele!

Now I'm anxious to parlay this experience into my true passion—sales. I love a challenge, I'm excited to learn and grow, and I want to do whatever it takes to be successful and contribute. I can't imagine a better place to do it than at Katz.

I truly hope to have the opportunity to talk about the Sales Assistant job in more detail. I'll plan to follow up in a week's time. In the meantime, feel free to contact me with any questions you may have.

Regards,

Justin Jackson
849.343.3433

Category 2:
How You Became Attracted to the Field

Return Address

Recipient Address

Dear Mr. Smith:

UBS gave me a taste of what the world of finance is all about. Now I'm looking for more.

I've been intrigued by the financial markets since my early teens when I steadfastly (and profitably) managed my own personal stock portfolio.

A finance minor at Cornell University piqued my interest further, and then I had a chance to work as an intern at UBS.

I made sales calls—certainly not the most glamorous job—but I worked hard and did a good job, and was able to bring in $70,000 worth of capital for my brokers. But more importantly I learned. I learned about the business, I learned about operations, and I learned about the markets.

My strengths are pretty clear. I love finance, I'm good at it, I work hard, and I get results. Whether it's sales calls or finance class, campus jobs or internships, I've made a difference throughout my life.

The institutional training program in services and operations at Merrill Lynch intrigues me. I'd love to be a part of an amazing program at a world-renowned institution.

I look forward to touching base with you soon.

Regards,

Christopher Couvillion
358.289.0493

Return Address

Recipient Address

Dear Ms. Smith:

They say variety is the spice of life.

Without a doubt, that's why I'm attracted to public relations.

Everything in the field is about variety. There are so many projects to work on simultaneously; there are so many clients and advertisers to work with. The job is analytical and strategic; it's also creative and executional.

I don't know everything about what it's like to work full-time in an agency, but I do know that every day will be different.

I had the opportunity to spend some time shadowing employees at a few agencies. I saw firsthand the "controlled chaos" that exists, and I know that's precisely the environment I'd thrive in.

I look forward to speaking with you in more detail about Edelman PR and any opportunities you may have available. I'll plan to follow up with you in about a week.

Regards,

Edith Eve
232.558.3436

Return Address

Recipient Address

Dear Ms. Smith:

In essence, one can relate so much of what has and what is going on in the world through economics and finance.

The History of the United States through the Economy was a class I took in college that really cemented my interest in finance. It was fascinating to learn how so much of our society is traced back to the economy and to economic endowments. It was then I knew that this was my passion.

I sincerely enjoy the field of finance. I'm intrigued by numbers, math, and puzzles. It's a discipline that's solution focused, and while it can be subjective, it's ultimately rooted in objectivity.

I look forward to the chance to learn more about opportunities at TRU Finance. I'll plan to follow up in a week's time.

Regards,

Blaine Billot
343.898.3405

Return Address

Recipient Address

Dear Ms. Smith:

Most people start studying advertising in college, but I got my start when I was 10 years old.

It all began in Mrs. Hogan's 4th grade classroom, when my teacher explained to us how the entertaining commercials we watched on Saturday morning television were actually designed to make us try Lucky Charms or a Happy Meal. Ever since, I've been fascinated by the power of advertising to affect attitudes and behavior.

Whenever and wherever possible, I've sought out opportunities to learn more about the business. While at Ohio University, I had the chance to work on nationally recognized advertising projects for Toyota and Bank of America as part of the AAF's National Student Advertising Competition. I can't tell you how exciting it was to see my ideas and my work come to life in front of judges and company executives. I'm now ready to parlay my experience into a full-time creative position at Element 79.

I'd love the opportunity to talk in more detail about my passion for advertising and to share some of my creative work with you. I look forward to speaking with you soon.

Regards,

Meredith Markers
909.340.7869

Return Address

Recipient Address

Dear Ms. Smith:

Financial markets have a profound impact on virtually every aspect of the world we live in. That's why I've set my sights on a career in the banking industry.

The complex connections that exist between the U.S. economy, international markets, and world events simply fascinate me. My course work in Economics and International Studies has served to strengthen my appreciation.

The more I've learned about these subjects over the past four years, the more I've wanted to know. My special interest in investment banking crystallized last summer at Wake Forest University's Summer Management Program, where I realized that the challenge, variety, and fast pace inherent in the business are a perfect match with my career aspirations.

I look forward to speaking with you in greater detail about the energy and enthusiasm I can bring to the U.S. Analyst position at Banc of America Securities. I'll plan to follow up with you in a week's time.

Regards,

Mara Malone
949.384.948

Category 3:
Some Interesting Experience
Related to the Field

Return Address

Recipient Address

Dear Mr. Smith:

As an administrative/operational guru, and as someone passionate about Christian music, I'm extremely intrigued by the Executive Assistant position within the CMG Label Group.

I'm one of those people who simply love getting things done. Whether it's everyday administrative tasks, coordinating work for large groups, or planning and executing events and projects, I truly thrive in that environment.

I also am practically addicted to Christian music. I'm a street rep on my campus for several labels and have coordinated music at retreats throughout the country. In fact, my friends describe me as a Christian music junkie!

I genuinely hope to have the opportunity to speak with you more about this Executive Assistant position and will plan to contact you in a week.

Regards,

Allison Aldridge
435.343.3432

Return Address

Recipient Address

Dear Ms. Smith:

The backbone of a successful sales organization is the people.

I know products like Powerade, Coca-Cola, and Sprite have extraordinary brand recognition, but to think that these products "sell themselves" is naïve.

I'm passionate about working with people to accomplish the task at hand. Whether starting and growing Miami's first clay target club, or working with a partner to place 5th in the state of Ohio for DECA, I'm certain that selling and networking are my greatest strengths.

Of most importance though was the perspective of the people I met from Coca-Cola. The way they talked about the company and the job and the experience convinced me that this is the ideal organization for me.

I look forward to following up about the Summer Sales Intern position and hope to touch base soon.

Regards,

Sarah Shoemaker
893.267.8932

Return Address

Recipient Address

Dear Mr. Smith:

Translating is a bit like solving a puzzle. All the pieces are there, and it's just a question of putting them together in the perfect order.

Translating is a challenge that keeps me constantly stimulated. And I'm the kind of person that craves challenges. I spent six years as a nationally ranked freestyle skier. The competition, the practice, and the team camaraderie all motivated me to excel.

I fell in love with translating when I took my first Japanese class. After studying the language at one of the top undergraduate Japanese programs in the country, I interned at a company in Japan this past summer to immerse myself full-time. I knew right then that translation was the career for me.

I recently took the Japanese Language Proficiency Test (JLPT) and am anxious to convert my translation passion into a full-time job. I look forward to talking more with you about opportunities at C & P International. I'll plan to follow up in a week.

Regards,

Fran Farmer
894.378.2945

Return Address

Recipient Address

Dear Ms. Smith:

Student Body Treasurer at the University of Tennessee and Documentary Photographer in Romania.

As far back as I can remember, I've been fascinated by both the analytical and the creative. If you look at my resume, you'll see a healthy dose of both sides of my brain.

I'm sure that's why market research in particular appeals to me.

I had a great taste of research life during an internship at the Iona Group. I worked as the primary liaison between a research firm and our CEO to create a Web site survey to launch a new technology product. I had a chance to then try to sell the product to the likes of Manchester United, the Kansas City Chiefs, and major national record labels. I loved it!

I'm extremely intrigued by the research at Creative Solutions, and I'd love to learn more.

I hope to have a chance to speak with you soon about any openings you may have. I'll plan on touching base in about a week.

Regards,

Brentley Barry
217.577.7434

Return Address

Recipient Address

Dear Ms. Smith:

Most people want to get away from the small towns they grew up in. I actually am dying to get back!

What attracts me to a small town is basically the same thing that attracts me to the field of marketing. I love people. I love getting to know them. And I love to help shape their behavior. Whether it's trying to sell laundry detergent to consumers around the country or trying to make friends in Lovington, IL, that's what it's all about.

I had a chance to hone my marketing skills at the University of Kentucky—a decidedly big school! I was part of the presentation team for the Florida Department of Tourism that competed against more than 150 teams across the country. We came in first in our regional and 16th in the nation at this prestigious competition.

With an advertising internship, lots of experience from classroom work, and some hands-on experience from my jobs, I know what it takes to make an impact and be successful. Now I'm excited to parlay my experience into a full-time job at Solutions, Inc.

I hope to touch base soon. I'll plan to contact you in a week.

Regards,

Elizabeth Elliot
217.835.9345

Category 4:
A Great Opportunity You Had

Return Address

Recipient Address

Dear Ms. Smith:

Juggling, working with a diverse group of teammates, project management, strategic skills, and a taste for the creative.

That's what makes a great account person. That's what I love about advertising.

I've been fortunate enough to have had some wonderful advertising experiences. I worked as an advertising intern on brands like Kraft, Clorox, and Diagio. Like any good intern, I had the opportunity to work on a variety of projects across several departments. Those juggling skills sure came in handy! It really made me realize the breadth of knowledge needed to be successful in the field.

Mothers Against Drunk Driving had me develop and create marketing materials for them as part of my involvement in the American Marketing Association while in school. I also was tapped to launch a Web site for another student group. Finally, my marketing classes taught me the hard skills necessary to tackle a job in account management.

I'm interested in parlaying my background into a career in advertising at DDB. I hope we have a chance to touch base soon. I'll plan on contacting you in about a week.

Regards,

Liza Lambert
309.556.9484

Return Address

Recipient Address

Dear Mr. Smith:

Nothing is as exciting as getting ready for game day.

The players warming up, the buzz of the crowd as it enters the park, even the smell of the stadium, all make for an electrically charged atmosphere. I've seen it firsthand and I love it.

I've been around professional sports since I was a child. My father worked as a Major League Baseball scout for more than 35 years. Even more importantly, I had the pleasure of spending this past summer as an intern for the Joliet JackHammers minor league baseball team.

It was an amazing experience. I interned in the Public/Media Relations department and had a chance to try my hand at an incredible variety of projects. I worked with ESPN as they covered the play of Pete Rose Jr. and a Cubs/Sox Legends game. I handled all our player appearances. I even set up and ran our first baseball camp. I usually put in 80 hours a week and couldn't get enough!

The JackHammers experience, in addition to work for the Chicago Bears and my Sports Management major, all have me extremely interested in pursing a career as a public relations assistant upon graduation.

I would love to talk with you more about my passion, my background, and your organization. I look forward to touching base with you soon.

Regards,

Lisa Szabo
708.394.5993

Return Address

Recipient Address

Dear Ms. Smith:

I'm glad we had the chance to talk about the Relationship Manager Development Program. As you know, I'm extremely interested in entering the world of finance upon graduation.

My background is unlike typical college students. I had the good fortune of working year-round as a Director of Business Operations for a $3.5MM medical services company with 18 full-time employees. In my five years there, I fundamentally altered the way they conduct their business, saving the company in excess of $100,000 a year.

As the Director of Business Operations, I had a vast amount of responsibility in both financial analysis and operations. I was doing everything from establishing a competitive payroll structure to administering our 401(K) plan to completely overhauling the collections process. Not your typical college internship!

I'm extremely intrigued by your RMDP. It offers the training and the challenges that I am looking forward to taking on. I'll plan to follow up with you shortly about next steps.

Regards,

Summer Sanchez
281.694.9347

Category 5:
Extensive Background

Return Address

Recipient Address

Dear Mr. Smith:

To me politics is fast paced, edgy, and competitive (in a good way). That's why I'm passionate about politics and that's why I'm dying to get involved.

As you'll see from my resume, I have a wealth of experience in the field. I've worked for the House Majority Whip in Kentucky, I've been a campaign staffer, and I've held leadership positions in Student Government at the University of Kentucky.

I'll be in Washington next fall as a Political Management Masters student at George Washington and hope to join you at the Democratic Congressional Committee this summer.

I know the page job is not the most glamorous position on Capitol Hill, but to me it's not about glamour. It's about working hard, making a contribution, and getting involved. I'm energetic and eager to enter the field and willing to do whatever it takes to ultimately become successful.

I look forward to following up with you about the job and will plan to contact you in a week.

Regards,

Nancy Nijoka
837.945.0483

Return Address

Recipient Address:

Dear Mr. Smith:

Technology and business—it's what your Management Analyst position is all about, and it's where my passion lies.

I have a unique background. I have two degrees from the Honor's College at Michigan State University—one in Computer Science and one in Marketing.

I pursued these degrees for one simple reason. I love technology and I love business. For me my goal has always been to marry the two as a profession.

As you'll see from my background outside the classroom, I've had the chance to hone my technology consulting skills through a series of internships.

I've tested business processes and procedures, I've analyzed a client's business and built a Web site, and I've provided support for a team of 400 users. In short, I've been fortunate enough to use my technology skills in a results-oriented business environment.

A Management Analyst at Bearing Point represents the best of the best for me. I'm sure you'll see from my resume that I have the background and skills to be successful.

I look forward to touching base with you soon.

Regards,

Louie Lim
454.954.4592

Return Address

Recipient Address

Dear Mr. Smith:

I'm not your traditional account management candidate.

I have an MBA in strategic thinking, an associate's degree in advertising, and a BBA from one of the most prestigious French schools in the world. I'm fluent in both French and Arabic.

My diverse educational and cultural background has given me a well-rounded global perspective not found in most new hires.

As for business, I've done project work for brands like BMW and Sony in addition to all the typical expertise one gets from an MBA.

I'm now anxious to parlay my experiences into an opportunity to work on an international assignment either here or abroad. I can't imagine a better place to do that than at DDB.

I look forward to touching base soon. I'll plan to follow up with you in about a week.

Regards,

Maurise Montivideo
342.373.2372

Return Address

Recipient Address

Dear Ms. Smith:

Ultimately the people who need the most legal work are often the ones who can't afford it. It's for that reason that I have been drawn to working with indigents and why I am intrigued by the summer internship program with the Public Defender's Office.

I was fortunate to have had some wonderful learning experiences at Juvenile Defenders, doing everything from client interviews to field investigations—from motion work to courtroom preparation. This past winter break, I was elevated to a Certified Law Clerk, handling cases on behalf of juvenile defendants. It was an incredible experience.

My passion for the law is founded in my love of mathematics. I was a math major in college and find that the links between math and the law are manifold. They are both about logic, about distilling a complex problem to a simpler form, and about uncovering a solution when a situation seems unsolvable.

Now I'm anxious to parlay my experience and my passion into a summer internship in your office. I look forward to the chance to discuss my candidacy in person. I'll plan to follow up in a week's time.

Regards,

Casey Colridge
232.677.6575

Category 6:
A Personal Connection

Return Address

Recipient Address

Dear Mr. Smith:

Glyn Williams, a current Boeing employee, and Mike Rolfes, a former employee, both suggested I get in touch with you regarding a position as an aeronautical engineer.

Of course, it's always nice to hear about a company from its employees, but I knew about how great Boeing was long before I talked to Glyn and to Mike.

In an interesting coincidence or in a brilliant stroke of prognostication, I actually selected Boeing as a project for an Engineering Practicum class last year at Iowa State University. For a class project, I had to choose a company that I both admired and wanted to work for, and as fate would have it, that company was yours!

As an engineering and history double major, I've always been intrigued by the field of aeronautics. The notion of determining what drives successful progress, and then quantitatively acting on it, fascinates me. In talking with Glyn and Mike, I realized that there is no better place to practice this discipline than at Boeing.

I hope I have a chance to share my passion for Boeing and for engineering with you in the near future. I'll plan to follow up shortly.

Regards,

Lee Loehr
319.341.4360

Return Address

Recipient Address

Dear Ms. Smith:

I had the pleasure of meeting with Darren Kapelus who reinforced my passion for ads that work.

He told me that's important for any new employee at Ogilvy, and it's also the reason I'm so attracted to advertising.

To me, it's incredibly compelling to be in an industry where you can send a message that will affect people's behavior. Whether it's altering a perception with laughter, tears, or plain old awareness, advertising can truly change attitudes and drive change.

I saw this firsthand this past summer as an intern at Reebok. I helped with dozens of retail marketing efforts across the country and saw immediately the power of advertising.

Within advertising, it's account management that interests me the most. I love solving problems both big and small. Sometimes it's about a creative solution, sometimes it's an analytical one, but in a field like advertising it's always about the people too. As a detail-oriented organizer who also can see the bigger picture, I know I'd fit in well.

I'm particularly intrigued by the Ogilvy notion of 360-degree branding. With continual innovation and constant change, I often wonder if David Ogilvy would recognize the world of advertising today! That being said, I'm very interested in being a part of an industry that continues to evolve.

I hope to have the chance to discuss my passion for advertising in person and look forward to the chance to interview when you come to Wesleyan.

Regards,

Danielle Donalds
494.305.8943

INDEX

Page numbers in *italic* indicate figures.

ABOUT THE AUTHOR

Brad Karsh is the nation's foremost authority on landing your first job. He has been featured on CNN's *Paula Zahn Now* and CNBC and has been quoted in *The Wall Street Journal, Fortune, ABCnews.com*, the *Chicago Tribune*, and dozens of other media outlets, talking about what it takes for students to find the jobs of their dreams. His company, JobBound (www.jobbound.com) has helped thousands of students with resumes, cover letters, interviewing, and everything related to the job search.

As president of JobBound, Brad travels the country presenting at universities, colleges, and other student gatherings. He's delivered job-search workshops to thousands of students in more than twenty-five states.

Prior to starting JobBound, Brad worked for fifteen years at Leo Burnett advertising in Chicago—one of the world's largest advertising agencies. He left in late 2002 as VP/Director of Talent Acquisition. While at Burnett, Brad evaluated more than ten thousand resumes, interviewed more than one thousand college students, and hired hundreds of new grads.

Brad currently lives in Chicago with his wife, Lisa.